D1131311

Linda Christie, M.A., is president of the Associates of Tulsa, an organization development consulting firm. She is an Associate of Team Associates, Inc., which provides management training and development. She has more than eight years of experience in corporate personnel management and is owner/manager of A.M.S., an outdoor power product sales and service business. She uses microcomputers in her consulting and retail business and for writing.

Jess W. Curry, Jr., has an M.S. in computer science and is a data processing consultant for the Tulsa office of Arthur Young & Company. His fifteen years of experience in data processing include the supervision of a small buiness consulting group, advising clients on the use of small computers, and teaching seminars and computer courses. He has degrees from Oklahoma State University and Kansas State University.

LINDA GAIL CHRISTIE
JESS W. CURRY, JR.

THE ABCs OF MICROCOMPUTERS

A Computer Literacy Primer

A SPECTRUM BOOK

Prentice-Hall, Inc., Englewood Cliffs, New Jersey 07632

Library of Congress Cataloging in Publication Data

Christie, Linda Gail.
  The ABCs of microcomputers.

  "A Spectrum Book."
  Includes index.
  1. Microcomputers.   I. Curry, Jess W.   II. Title.
QA76.5.C485   1983   001.64   82-21507
ISBN 0-13-000620-3
ISBN 0-13-000612-2 (pbk.)

This book can be made available to businesses and organizations
at a special discount when ordered in large quantities.
Contact: Prentice-Hall, Inc.,
General Book Marketing, Special Sales Division,
Englewood Cliffs, New Jersey 07632

© 1983 by Prentice-Hall, Inc., Englewood Cliffs, N.J. 07632

All rights reserved. No part of this book
may be reproduced in any form or
by any means without permission in writing
from the publisher.

Printed in the United States of America

1   2   3   4   5   6   7   8   9   10

ISBN 0-13-000620-3

ISBN 0-13-000612-2{pbk.}

Cover design by Hal Siegel. Manufacturing buyer: Cathie Lenard.

Prentice-Hall International, Inc., *London*
Prentice-Hall of Australia Pty., Limited, *Sydney*
Prentice-Hall of Canada, Ltd., *Toronto*
Prentice-Hall of India Private, Limited, *New Dehli*
Prentice-Hall of Japan, Inc., *Tokyo*
Prentice-Hall of Southeast Asia Pte., Ltd., *Singapore*
Whitehall Books, Limited, *Wellington, New Zealand*
Editora Prentice-Hall do Brasil Ltda., *Rio de Janeiro*

105601

BELMONT COLLEGE LIBRARY

QA
76.5
.C485
1983

To P.M. Fielding

CONTENTS

Preface   ix

I   **WHAT IS A MICROCOMPUTER?**

1   What Is a Microcomputer?   3

II   **WHAT DO MICROCOMPUTERS DO?**

2   101 Home Computer Applications   11
3   Microcomputers in the Classroom   25
4   101 Business Applications   35
5   Central Files: The Data Base Management
     Concept   49
6   Death of the Typewriter: The Word
     Processor   53

**III HOW TO SELECT
MICROCOMPUTER HARDWARE**

    7   The Limits of Internal Memory   65

    8   Secondary Storage: "Unlimited"
        Memory   73

    9   Selecting a Printer   83

   10   The Terminal Decision   91

   11   Hardware from Accumulator to VLSI   99

**IV HOW TO SELECT
MICROCOMPUTER SOFTWARE**

   12   Software Isn't So Hard   109

   13   How to Evaluate Documentation
        Manuals   119

   14   Games Computers Play   129

   15   Evaluating Educational Software   135

   16   Programming Is Like Writing
        a Novel   145

   17   Which Language Is Best?   153

   18   Is Security Really a Problem?   161

   19   Software from Abort to Virtual
        Memory   167

V WHICH ONE IS BEST?

   20   Performing the Needs Analysis   173

   21   Putting It All Together   183

Glossary   191

Index   211

PREFACE

Learning about microcomputers is perhaps one of the most interesting opportunities we have today. Numerous books have been written by computer professionals with the express purpose of helping the layperson understand this new technology. Why then should you spend your time reading this book versus all of the others? How is it different? And what can you expect to get out of this book once you've completed reading it?

Unlike most introductory microcomputer texts, *The ABCs of Microcomputers* doesn't approach the technical information until Chapter 7. Beginning chapters such as "101 Home Computer Applications," "Microcomputers in the Classroom," and "101 Business Applications" stimulate your thinking and help you identify how you can use a microcomputer.

Practical "how-to" chapters such as "Selecting a Printer," "The

Terminal Decision," "How to Evaluate Documentation," and "Putting It All Together" provide easy, step-by-step guidance through the microcomputer maze.

All technical terms are defined as they appear in the text and in the Glossary at the end of each chapter. You won't be overwhelmed and you won't get lost. The quick-reference Glossary and the Index provide rapid access to any term which might cause you trouble.

Because each chapter stands on its own, you can skip the technical chapters and move on to material which you may prefer to read. Home users, small business users, and educators will find that *The ABCs of Microcomputers* addresses the needs of the novice in a language and style they can understand and enjoy.

For those of you who wish to learn microcomputer jargon, this book, with its extensive Glossary of microcomputer terms, also presents the complex concepts. Chapters such as "The Limits of Internal Memory," "Which Language is Best?" and "Hardware from Accumulator to VLSI" address topics for the reader interested in "what makes it tick."

The ABCs of Microcomputers, written in simple everyday English, which discusses applications, equipment, programming, and operations of microcomputers. This book provides the computer novice an effective, interesting, and organized system for learning this new technology.

ABCs is a layperson's guide to microcomputer literacy terms that provides a real alternative to the technically written texts on the market.

WHAT IS A MICROCOMPUTER?

1

WHAT IS A
MICROCOMPUTER?

"Dad, what's a microcomputer?" The freckled youngster looked up at his parent.

If you haven't faced this question yet, it's only a matter of time. Parents, teachers, small business owners, housewives, and professionals will all encounter the microcomputer in the next two to four years.

Perhaps Phil Jones' explanation to his daughter Tracy will give some insights into what this new technology means to us:

"A microcomputer is a machine that does arithmetic at very high speeds." Her father drew a circle on the page.

"Like a calculator?"

"Actually a calculator is a small computer. A key difference is that microcomputers can be instructed to do more than a calculator. The instructions the computer user gives a computer are called a *program* or *software.*" He completed the drawing.

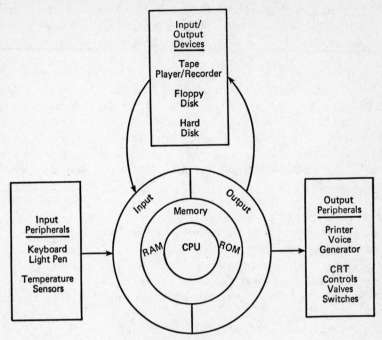

FIGURE 1–1. The microcomputer

"What're those circles and squares?" Tracy pointed to the sketch.

"This large circle represents the CPU or *Central Processing Unit.* The CPU does arithmetic, makes comparisons, and performs logical functions. As the heart of the computer system, the CPU controls all operations. That's one reason it needs a *clock.* Each process must be done at the right time and in the right order."

"Can a computer remember?" Tracy pointed to the ring labeled *memory.*

"There are two basic types of memory in a computer. RAM or *Random-Access Memory* is used by the computer like you might use a scratch pad to remind yourself of calculations you had done on a math problem. RAM can be *erased* by telling the computer to forget it or by turning the computer off."

He continued, "ROM or *Read-Only Memory* normally is not erasable and not alterable by programming. ROM contains the basic instructions a computer needs to operate, like the instructions our brain has for breathing, regulating our heart beat, and waking up. ROM controls the functions basic to the computer's existence as a useful device."

"I see, the CPU is like our brain," Tracy said.

"There are many similarities. Like our brain, the CPU can't do much without sensing the outside world. We have eyes, ears, and fingers that bring our brain information from the outside. The computer uses *input peripherals* to send messages by electrical signals to its brain, the CPU, and to provide instructions or data."

"The *user,* or person using the computer, types instructions and data on the *keyboard,*" he continued. "The CRT or *Cathode Ray Tube* takes the place of paper in the typewriter. The TV-type screen shows the user the information just typed on the keyboard. When the user pushes the *enter* or *return* key on the keyboard, the information travels from the *terminal (keyboard* and CRT) through wires to the CPU for processing."

"Is the terminal the only contact the CPU has with the outside world?" Tracy asked.

"There are several other common data sources," he answered. "For example, the user may want to *load* or give to the CPU a long program or a large file of information that's already written. The file or program is stored on *cassette tape* or *floppy diskette.* The *cassette tape player/recorder* is just like the one you play your favorite music on. *Floppy disks* are soft disks made from material similar to magnetic tape. The user *inputs* the information from these records or *auxiliary memories* into RAM so the computer can use the data."

"How does the computer talk?" Tracy asked.

"When the computer has the solution to the problem or wants to ask for more information, it sends a message through wires to the terminal, *printer,* or memory storage device. *Output* is the information generated by the computer and sent to an *output peripheral.* The user can read the output on the CRT or on the *printer.* The printer is like a fast typewriter with no keyboard. The printer is controlled by the CPU."

"I see." Tracy picked up the colorful brochure, "The input peripherals, the CPU, and the output peripherals all make up the complete *computer system.*"

"That's it in a nutshell. We're going to use microcomputers more and more in the next ten years. Want to help me find one?"

GLOSSARY

Cassette. A tape recorder/player and magnetic tape cartridge used to input information to or record output information from the CPU.

Clock. A device in the CPU which is used as an internal time reference for controlling operations.

Console. An input device resembling a typewriter and ten-key keyboard used to type information into the CPU.

CPU (Central Processing Unit). The heart of the microcomputer that performs the arithmetic and logic functions; controls all of the operations; and controls the memory.

CRT (Cathode Ray Tube). A peripheral device resembling a TV screen that displays input and output information to the user.

Disk Drive. A device that spins the diskette and electrically reads and writes information on it.

Diskette. A flexible disk made of magnetic tape material used for storing information.

Enter Key. A key on the console keyboard that, when pushed, causes the data typed by the user to be transferred through wires to the CPU.

Erase. To remove data from memory.

Floppy Disk. See *Diskette.*

Hard Copy. A slang term for the printed material produced by a computer.

Input. Noun: Information put into the computer. Verb: To put information into the computer.

Input Peripheral. Devices such as terminals, light pens, temperature sensors, disk drives, cassette tape players, and ten-key pads that send information to the CPU.

Load. The process of putting data or programs into the CPU from a disk or cassette.

Microcomputer. A small computer.

Memory. The capability a computer has for retaining information.

Output. Noun: Information generated by the computer and communicated through wires to an output device. Verb: To send out information from the computer.

Output Peripheral. Devices such as terminals, CRTs, cassette tape recorders, disk drives, printers, control devices (valves, thermostats), and voice generators that receive information from the CPU for the user to utilize.

Peripheral. An input or output device connected by wires to the CPU, used to send or receive information. See *Input Peripheral* and *Output Peripheral.*

Printer. A typewriter-type device that makes a hard copy of the data, programs, or communications from the CPU. It is operated by the computer and may have a keyboard of its own.

Program. Noun: A set of instructions that tells the computer what to do. Verb: To write the instructions for the computer.

Programmer. One who writes instructions for the computer.

RAM (Random-Access Memory). A place in the computer that is capable of recording information for use in calculations and comparisons. It serves as a scratch pad to remind the computer of what it has done and to record data. RAM is erasable by instructions or by turning the computer off.

Return Key. See *Enter Key.*

ROM (Read-Only Memory). A place in the CPU that provides the computer's basic instructions for functioning. Programming and turning the computer off doesn't alter ROM.

Software. See *Program.*

Terminal. See *Console.*

User. A person who uses computer-generated information or reports.

WHAT DO MICROCOMPUTERS DO?

2

101 HOME COMPUTER APPLICATIONS

Originally people thought the home computer was an expensive toy. Since the prices have decreased and the software has improved, people are beginning to see how a home computer can improve their quality of life.

With the addition of telecommunications which connect the micro-computer to two-way cable television and other computers, the capabilities for home computers seem limited only by the owner's imagination and resourcefulness.

A ROMANTIC INTERLUDE

Renaldo stroked the straying strands of black hair from his forehead. He remained calm even though Carmalita was due any moment. The doorbell rang to announce her arrival. The lights dimmed, soft music slowly filled the room, and the coffeepot began to sizzle.

Renaldo pressed the combination on the keypad beside the door and as the door swung aside, her perfume caressed his nostrils.

"Hello," she said. Her dark eyes sparkled, "I hope dinner is ready, I'm starved."

"Let me take your coat." He took the fur from her shoulders, "Is it still snowing?"

She rubbed her hands together and blew her warm breath on the reddened fingers, "A little. Can you turn up the heat?"

"It's already done," he said placing the coat in the closet. "This time of year Margarita does it automatically when the door opens."

She swung around toward him, "You have another woman here?"

Renaldo smiled, "Woman? Well, I guess you could say she's my housekeeper." He laughed at the puzzled look on Carmalita's face, "No, not another woman. Margarita is my microcomputer."

"Your what?"

"Come, let me introduce you to her." Renaldo led Carmalita toward the television screen on his desk, "Carmalita, meet Margarita."

"I'm afraid I don't understand." She cocked her head to get a better look at the contraption. "This doesn't look like it can keep house."

"Oh, but you're wrong." He grinned, "She starts coffee for me in the morning, makes sure I get out of bed, turns up the heat so I don't freeze, turns on the morning news on the television, and even prints out a grocery list for me." He patted the terminal tenderly, "I don't know what I'd do without her."

Sound a little far-fetched? Not really. Microcomputers are improving the quality of life for many people. By connecting sensors that detect temperature, for example, the microcomputer can regulate the heating and air-conditioning systems. It can even detect when a room is not being used and direct minimal energy to that area.

Enter the time and channel for each of your favorite television shows and the computer will alternate between them and your favorite FM radio station. Rather look at the Christmas slides or movies of the children? The microcomputer will lower the screen from the ceiling, close the venetian blinds, draw the drapes, dim the lights, and control the projector. Connect it to your videotape recorder and create your own graphics, cartoons, and titles. Show the production on your large screen color television.

Many parties liven up with computer games. There is no need to go to the expensive arcade, just play in your living room. With cable television and a home computer, hundreds of games "fill your library." Games to test your wits, eye-hand coordination, and ingenuity, and lots of sheer fun are at your fingertips.

Don't like crowds? Play alone. Let the microcomputer be your chess or bridge partner.

VOLUNTEER TO BE THE
ORGANIZATION SECRETARY

Think I'm crazy? Sometimes people want to contribute to an organization but just don't seem to have the time. Of all the jobs, taking minutes, keeping track of the membership list, and mailing correspondence seems to be the most demanding. But not with a microcomputer!

Just enter the mailing list one time. Update it occasionally with address changes or new members. But any time a newsletter or announcement needs to be sent, just press a button and the mailing labels are automatically printed. Need the labels in zip code order? Automatic. Need an alphabetical telephone list for all the members? The microcomputer makes it simple.

The newsletter? Enter it on the word processor. Make corrections and last minute entries. When you print it, you can even justify the right margin. It looks really professional. Ooops! Found a mistake after it was all typed? Just correct the mistake and have the computer reprint it in minutes.

The life of the organization secretary is greatly improved with the aid of the microcomputer.

SPECIAL DIETS
NO PROBLEM TO BALANCE

Just enter the name of the food, the number of calories per serving, and the nutritional data such as vitamin and mineral content, protein and carbohydrate levels, salt content, etc. By knowing the recommended daily levels for a weight reducing diet, low salt diet, low cholesterol diet etc., the cook can design menus for the week. Add height, weight, age, sex, and a factor for activity level and get a customized diet.

Check the menus for the week against your pantry inventory and create a grocery shopping list.

The drudgeries of the kitchen are lightened with a microcomputer.

WHO'LL WATER THE GARDEN WHILE WE'RE ON VACATION?

The microcomputer, of course. Microcomputers are perfectly suited for controlling valves. Just establish a watering schedule for the areas of the yard and garden and the microcomputer will follow your instructions while you hike in the Rockies.

No one knows how to get it to mow the grass yet, but I'm sure someone is working on it.

VOICE-CONTROLLED WHEEL CHAIRS

Many quadraplegics cannot reliably operate even the most simple "manual" or mechanical electric wheel chair control system. Microcomputers can "recognize" voice commands which cause the computer to operate switches on an electric wheel chair. In this way the quadraplegic is able to safely control mobility.

Some microcomputers are helping cerebral palsy victims speak for the first time in their lives. By controlling switches or a keyboard with their hands or feet, they activate a voice synthesizer which conveys their message. They can even converse in this manner over the telephone.

The role of microcomputers in improving the lives of physically and learning disabled people is just coming to light. As technology develops for other uses, researchers in the disability fields are using technological advances to meet their needs.

"THERE'S A BURGLARY IN PROGRESS AT . . ."

The microcomputer can detect intrusion and notify the police by telephone. Sensors placed in strategic entry points such as doors and windows or in pathways such as halls send signals to the microcomputer. The computer responds to their warning by dialing the police and playing a recorded message which tells where the burglary is in progress.

THE LIBRARY OF CONGRESS
IN YOUR LIVING ROOM

With a microcomputer and telecommunications (possibly through cable television) you will be able to search through library computers anywhere in the world.

"Mom, why do animals have black noses and we don't?" Ever had a question like that from a four-year-old? Now you can find the answer in minutes. That is, providing you know how to look up "black noses."

COMPUTER SUMMER CAMPS FOR KIDS

After the horseback riding and canoeing, it's time for "playing" with the microcomputer. Children can engage in games, models, simulations, skill drills, competitions, problem solving, designing, programming, and anything else they can dream up. And it keeps them off the streets.

NO MORE STAMPS

Electronic mail with microcomputers is a reality. Even now with the use of word processing and telecommunications, messages can be rapidly transmitted great distances over telephone lines. At the other end, the receiving microcomputer prints out the letter or contract, letter perfect.

Soon satellite transmission will be available, or large computers may forward messages to their destination. Who said a computer never reads its mail?

WHO'LL WIN THE SUPERBOWL?

Now you can make predictions on the outcomes of horse races, college basketball games, professional football games, and even roulette and other games of chance.

Develop your own betting system. Enter the horse genealogy and analyze your odds. Develop a system for managing your money.

Don't want to play with real money? Keep score on the computer.

WRITE THAT TUNE

Microcomputers have software available that allows the user to write and edit music just like a word processor allows the writing of text. Instead of having a printer, the computer has a music synthesizer attached. This electronic device is capable of duplicating the sounds and intonation of many musical instruments as well as uncommon sounds. It plays chords or single notes.

The composer hears immediately how the combination of notes sounds. With quick editing, another bar is tried.

CONTROL YOUR EMOTIONS

Connect electrodes to parts of your body that send signals to the microcomputer about your pulse rate, blood pressure, galvanic skin responses (tenseness), and respiration. The computer will plot a graph or send an audible signal to you indicating your level of tension. For example, a high-pitched tone might indicate a high level of tension and a low tone relaxation.

Concentrate on lowering the tone. Your body will respond to your commands and the biofeedback from the microcomputer will tell you what works for you.

WHEN ARE YOU AT YOUR BEST?

Some researchers feel that a biorhythm chart indicates the times of the month that you are at your peak of physical energy and fitness.

Some people regulate their activities according to their chart, which is based on their birth date information. Create your own chart and study the relationships. If they work for you, use them to your advantage.

STARGAZERS MOVE IN TIME

With computerized models of the universe, stargazers can identify the stars, planets, visible galaxies, and constellations in the night sky. If the amateur astronomer wants to see what the universe looks like from

Alpha Centauri (our nearest neighboring star), the computer will show the sky from that vantage point.

If the user wants to see what the constellations looked like 2 thousand years ago (or 2 million years ago) from earth, the computer model will "run back" the clock to that night sky in the past.

BUY, SELL, OR SIT TIGHT?

Making commodity, bonds, and stock market decisions is a tricky and expensive proposition. With a microcomputer the task of analyzing and tracking data and trends is much easier. The computer can even compare historical information useful in the decision processes.

Portfolio monitoring, price watching, technical analysis, and fundamental analysis are all done in hours instead of days. You can even use Standard and Poor's monthly common-stock data service on your own microcomputer.

SAVE ON FUEL BILLS

The microcomputer is able to control the distribution of heat and air conditioning throughout your home. By sensing the outside and inside temperature, the computer adjusts the thermostat to optimize energy costs.

The computer can perform an energy analysis so you can decide whether to increase your insulation, install storm windows, or make other modifications in your home.

Solar heating systems are controlled with microcomputers. Valves regulate the circulation of hot water. Even the angle and direction of solar panels are controlled to optimize their effectiveness.

PAY YOUR BILLS ELECTRONICALLY

Want to know what your current bank balance is? Want to transfer $500 from savings to checking to cover an overdraft? Want to pay your utility bills? With a microcomputer and telecommunications you can do these operations and more at home.

The microcomputer, either through telephone lines or cable television lines, can communicate with the bank's computer. You can make inquiries about your accounts as well as control transactions. With two-way communication, the bank can even answer your questions. The day of the paper check may be drawing to a close. Money may someday exist only as electrical signals and memory messages in computers. Eventually stores will transfer money from your checking account to pay for a purchase before you leave the store. If you forget your wallet, you'll still be able to make a purchase.

PUBLIC INFORMATION AT YOUR FINGERTIPS

Want to check on a deed at the courthouse? When is the next city commission meeting? Is your divorce final?

When microcomputers communicate with city, state, and other public computers, a wealth of information will be available.

Want a library book delivered in the mail? Just look up the information in the public library's computerized card catalog, check it out, and it will be delivered by the mail carrier.

SHOULD YOU PAY OFF THAT LOAN EARLY?

Your mortgage payments are $500 per month for the next twenty years. When would it be paid if you paid $525 per month instead? How much interest would you save? Would inflation eat up the difference?

The microcomputer allows you to vary these factors until you find the payment plan that best meets your needs.

GAMES, GAMES, GAMES!

Make all of your dreams and fantasies come true with a microcomputer and some good game software. The variety of games is endless: war and space simulation, board games, sports, gambling and card games, shoot-em-up games, arcade style games, puzzle and strategy games, personal enlightenment, entertainment, art and music composition.

Fantasy and adventure games are role-playing games that require quick wits. You are the eyes and hands of the knight in shining armor or the treasure hunter. A hoard of ghosts, dragons, and pirates thwart your progress through a maze until the princess is saved or the treasure is found.

War and space simulation games test your strategy and sharp-shooting skills. Spaceships, airplanes, and other targets elude your pursuit. Explosions, surprise attacks, and the environment keep you, the commander, alert and struggling.

For the more sedate player, board games provide stiff competition. Monopoly, poker, hearts, backgammon, chess, checkers and other popular games keep you and your friends entertained and challenged for hours.

Gambling and card games such as craps, roulette, crazy eights, bridge, and solitaire lend themselves well to computer simulation.

Bowling, tennis, basketball, baseball, boxing, football, and golf give the armchair sports fan an opportunity to defeat the greatest quarterback or the top tennis pro. No sore muscles or bruises either.

Personal enlightenment programs allow you to develop your horoscope, to predict the future with ancient tarot, to study biorhythms, to compose music, and to "draw" computer graphics in color.

Game software outsells any other type of software available for microcomputers. Computer games provide many hours of entertainment.

HOME INVENTORY

Keep a record of your valuables, furnishings, etc. for insurance purposes. Be certain to store a printed copy off the premises (for example, in your safety deposit box) in case your house blows or floats away with your microcomputer.

The list is easily maintained by editing it as purchases are made or items removed.

PREPARE SKILLS INVENTORY

Put information on all of the church members into a skills inventory, and when particular expertise is required you'll know whom to call first. The editing capabilities facilitate updating. Need to print a mailing list to solicit contributions? The microcomputer makes the task an easy one.

INCOME TAX BLUES?

Let your microcomputer do your taxes. Enter the data and specify how the computer should compute tax liability. For example, you may want to see if income averaging would improve your financial picture.

Want to know if you should make another tax-deductible contribution before the end of the year? Alter your data and see what effect it has. If your taxes are lower, you may want to take action before the year is over.

CAN'T BALANCE YOUR CHECKBOOK?

Your microcomputer can do it with ease and accuracy. Just enter the checks you've written and deposits you've made and let the computer do the rest. What a relief!

NO EXCUSE FOR NOT WRITING

Now there's no excuse for not keeping up with your correspondence with family and friends. You just write the information you wish to tell everyone on your word processor and then customize each letter by adding a personal message. After it's printed on the printer, no one will know you didn't write the whole thing for them alone.

You don't need a skilled typist since you can make instant corrections with your word processor. The printer types a neat and accurate letter every time.

THE GREAT AMERICAN NOVEL

Many people dream of writing the great American novel, or they may want to write poetry or detective stories. The word processing capabilities of microcomputers not only increase the writers' productivity, but also improve the quality of their manuscripts. Greater care is taken to edit each page so that just the right word or phrase is used. There is no problem in changing just one verb to make the impact more powerful. With a typewriter, that type of correction might mean retyping an entire page.

When the manuscript is printed with a word-processing printer it looks beautiful to the publisher's weary eyes. He'll pick your manuscript from the pile and read it first.

This book, for example, was submitted on floppy disk which saved typing expense and time.

GROW A FAMILY TREE

Those who study their family genealogy find that a microcomputer stores and catalogs the information in an organized, retrievable fashion. Adding a piece of information in the correct place is simple. Printing out the materials is done with a push of a button.

GRADES SLIPPING?

When the teacher asks for help, sometimes children resist being drilled by their parents. Does your child need to practice addition of the numbers 1–10? The microcomputer will work tirelessly with the youngster, will keep "score," and will give immediate reinforcement as to whether the answer is correct.

Microcomputers most likely won't replace teachers, but they can make their job easier.

THE AGE OF COMPUTER LITERACY

When today's youngsters grow up, they will live in a computer world. More and more jobs and activities revolve around or interface with computers of all sizes.

Exposure at a young age to microcomputers and computer terminology reduces apprehension and creates a positive atmosphere for learning. Even the simplest computer games teach the youngster (or adult) the basics of computer operations.

Many home computer owners find pleasure from programming their microcomputers. The challenge of learning a language and system of logic, of making the program work, and of creating a game or utilitarian application provides hours of pleasure for the microcomputer hobbiest-programmer.

Clubs called "user groups" attract microcomputer hobbiests who share their frustrations, achievements, and knowledge with their fellows. Software trades between user groups in different cities make games and other programs available at very low costs.

Monthly meetings feature speakers who share their experiences as users and tell the group how they can get more out of their current systems.

The comradery between microcomputer users develops quickly. A peculiar bond forms rapidly between users of microcomputers. The microcomputer may fill an important social function by bringing people together.

The home computer can no longer be considered an expensive luxury. Counting the microprocessors used in watches, calculators, children's toys, automobiles, and microwaves, to mention only a few, there will be at least five microprocessors per household by 1990.

3

MICROCOMPUTERS
IN THE CLASSROOM

Educators and business training professionals are feeling the pressures of having to learn a new technology to stay abreast in their profession. Just as we all strained to learn the "new math" in the sixties, another major change in education is coming from microcomputers in the classrooms.

School administrators, teachers, professors, parents, executives, and training specialists are all examining the educational potential of microcomputers. Most are beginning with limited budgets and are cautious not to move ahead without preparation and experimentation.

These budget restrictions unfortunately create unnecessary limitations on the uses and returns the microcomputers can deliver. The results will be limited since the investment is small. Nothing ventured, nothing gained.

However, caution *should* be taken. Nothing is more discouraging to schools, parents, and businesses than investing thousands of dollars in equipment only to find it stored in the closet. For example, companies invested millions in video equipment in the seventies. And, today, due to poor planning and training of personnel in the use of the equipment, dust gathers on the cameras and monitors.

START WITH A NEEDS ANALYSIS

Performing a needs analysis and planning how the microcomputers are to be used are the first tasks educators and trainers should address.

Identifying realistic objectives and goals is not enough. Practical steps for achieving end results must be developed before change will occur. Saying that the microcomputer will be used by the Mathematics Department for skill building is inadequate. Building what kind of skills? For what grade? Which children? Which teachers? When? And, why?

Companies face the same problems. What software is available to accomplish the learning objectives? Will special programs have to be written? Who will write the programs? What will software and staff development cost? And most important, what's the bottom line?

The needs analysis defines the uses and details the measures by which the microcomputer educational program can be evaluated after implementation. Such an evaluation will justify or prevent the expenditures of additional monies in automated learning.

ELEMENTARY SCHOOL: COMPUTER LITERACY

When funds and equipment are limited, drill and practice is a poor way to get results. Since many computer hours are required to produce skill development, large amounts of keyboard time must be available.

In response, some schools have decided to use drill and practice routines with learning disabled or exceptionally bright children. They feel that concentrating limited computer time on these youngsters will bring the most benefit.

However, other schools feel that all children should have equal access to the new technology. Computer literacy courses don't make high demands on computer time. The students get hands-on experience as well as a framework of information to understand the new science.

In a computer literacy course the students are taught such subjects as base-2 math, the history of computers, computer capabilities, general hardware configurations, and keyboard operations. This exposure prepares them for moving into the more complex concepts and applications.

JUNIOR HIGH SCHOOL: APPLICATIONS AND PROBLEM SOLVING

The junior high program in many school systems explores the applications for computers and microcomputers in our society. Career opportunities in the computer fields and an introduction to programming principles are covered. Also, the students have an opportunity to solve problems on the computer using these skills.

The computer also aids the teachers in demonstrating mechanical concepts and mathematical principles through modeling and simulation techniques. There is nothing like a moving picture on the screen to show which way gears and pulleys will turn or how much leverage a mechanical design will exert.

SENIOR HIGH SCHOOLS: COMPLEX USAGE AND SKILL DEVELOPMENT

The senior high schools expand the student's knowledge and skills in data processing. Computer science, electronics and hardware courses, software development courses, and business computer applications are explored in more depth and at a more sophisticated level.

Flowcharting, text editing, graphics and animation, programming, and problem solving are easily mastered before college.

COLLEGES AND UNIVERSITIES

Currently, institutions of higher education are performing at the levels we've described for public school. Eventually, though, time won't be spent on literacy and microcomputer orientation. Microcomputers will be used as tools by students and professors alike.

The biology lab will use microcomputers to control experiments and to monitor and analyze results. Students will write or modify programs to establish the experimental conditions and to manipulate the data.

Sociology departments will use microcomputers to simulate social conditions. "What if" exercises will demonstrate the effects of changing conditions on the social norms. For example, "What if the population of New York City doubled?" or, "What if people retired at 70 instead of 65?"

The business school will use the microcomputer to help students understand the interrelationships between factors on the company balance sheet. Students will be able to answer questions like, "What happens to profits if sales increase 20 percent?" and, "What happens to production costs if the minimum wage increases $1.30?"

Professors will use microcomputers to construct tests, to perform item analyses, and to keep performance records. The class performance statistics will be calculated and compared with previous years to check proficiency levels. Student records are retained and accumulated throughout the semester so final grades are calculated in minutes. The microcomputer then will transfer the data to the central mainframe computer for posting of transcripts.

BUSINESS AND MILITARY TRAINING DEPARTMENTS: SKILL TRAINING AND MANAGEMENT DEVELOPMENT

Simulators have been used for years to train pilots and astronauts. Now microcomputers provide the same advantage to skill development training at affordable prices.

Training a tank gunner with real tanks and shells is expensive. With a microcomputer the trainee develops and practices eye-hand coordination, siting, and other skills directly applicable to field performance.

Pulling the best mechanic off of the production line to be a trainer lowers productivity and often doesn't meet the career needs of the mechanic. In the future, the mechanic will participate only in the course content design. The instruction will be carried out by the microcomputer, while the mechanic returns to his duties. His expertise, however, will be shared with hundreds of workers simultaneously.

Trainers and management development specialists use microcomputers in management assessment exercises to determine the abilities of personnel. By observing how the participants approach the solutions and how they justify their decisions with the microcomputer data, trainers become aware of talents and deficiencies. Training programs are designed to develop managers to perform at high skill levels.

COMPUTER GRAPHICS ILLUSTRATE AND IMPROVE ATTENTION

Microcomputers also assist training departments by creating and presenting graphics for meetings. "Slides" are created and edited with computer graphics. When the training presentation is ready, the microcomputer projects the "slide" on a wide-screen television.

Audience attention is enhanced with the addition of motion. The trainer adds facts to the slides as the presentation progresses. For example, a slide showing the increase in profits from year to year may be shown in progressive steps. From frame to frame the line climbs from peak to peak.

When the slide needs to be updated, it only takes a few minutes for the user to edit the old information stored in computer memory and project the current year's data.

AN OVERVIEW

Students can learn *from* microcomputers, learn *with* microcomputers, and learn *about* microcomputers. Computerized instruction, computer-managed instruction, problem solving, simulations, programming, strategies, and planning are all possible.

Computer Augmented Learning (CAL) is designed to solve "real world" problems. It's the easiest, cheapest instructional technique to implement. Much software exists and little instructor training is needed.

Computer Managed Instruction (CMI) assists the instructor in record keeping, diagnostic testing, test scoring, and planning future instruction.

Computer Assisted Instruction (CAI) presents the information to and interacts with the student to enhance learning. Simple drill and practice and sophisticated tutorial systems fall in this category. The microcomputer is the drillmaster and record keeper. CAI is only cost effective where educational costs are high, for example in medical schools, military training, and handicapped learning.

Computer Literacy teaches the students about microcomputers. Computer capabilities, limitations, implications for society, and functions are presented to prepare the students for working in the field or relating to computers on their jobs or at home.

Computer-Aided Adult Learning (CAAL) programs work with a different set of assumptions than CAI. CAAL promotes self-directed and self-designed learning strategies rather than group learning experiences led by a professional. The delivery system is responsive to the trainee's need to know and to time constraints. The lessons are highly modular and flexible for targeted learning. Individual pacing adjusts for variability in learning speed, which is often greater in adults.

The lessons engage the learner in dialog, monitor the learner's progress, provide a constant summary of material covered, and offer feedback on progress toward mastery.

The right to learn with privacy and dignity in a risk-free environment keeps adults from looking foolish. In private nobody can embarrass them, and the freedom from unnecessary stress increases the learning rate.

EDUCATIONAL APPLICATIONS

Here are some specific applications for microcomputers:

- Chemistry professors use microcomputers to teach chemical formulation. Accidents in the laboratory are avoided and the rate of learning is increased.
- Weather front simulation demonstrates to students weather concepts and frontal movements.
- Geographical shore features create a model of the seashore for students to study erosion, currents, and food production cycles.
- The mechanics of poetry, composition, and editing are handled as well as statistical analysis.
- Phonics taught by a microcomputer improves reading skills and provides practice on any structural or phonetic part of a word.
- Writing and typing with a word processor remove much of the drudgery caused by the typewriter as well as wasteful retyping. In fact, teaching word processing is a good way to demonstrate how "dumb" a computer really is. Keyboard skills should be taught in the third grade. Word processors help students keep up with pen pals and free them for creative writing tasks.
- Mechanical models show how gears, chains, belts, and pulleys work together in a simulated machine. Which way do they turn? How much leverage is created? What's a more efficient design?
- The student newspaper or the alumni news can be composed on a word processor.

- Music synthesizers and microcomputers work well together to compose music. The student can hear the series of notes or the chord immediately, change the notes, and listen again.

- Automechanic instructors use microcomputers to compute the effects of maintenance on gasoline mileage. What was the mileage before the tune-up? After? Maintenance records can be kept on vehicles with the computer alerting the user when the next oil change is due.

- Art students can create designs and color combinations as well as color "slide" graphics on microcomputers.

- Instructors use the microcomputer to compile attendance records for absences and tardiness. Patterns can be detected for individuals so remedial action might be taken.

- Foreign language tutoring to learn vocabularies, declensions, and parts of speech are drilled time and again with no impatience expressed by the tireless microcomputer.

- Drafting instructors can have their students design building structures with the microcomputer. Stresses and tolerances are tested to see if it will fall over.

- Interior decorators move walls and appliances on the microcomputer screen without hammers and smashed fingers. Maximizing space utilization and studying travel patterns is as easy as a push of the button.

- Scheduling classes each semester can be a nightmare. Who has already taken what? Who needs what course to graduate on time? How many youngsters have enrolled for Drama 101? What is the best time to teach biology? Are two classes scheduled for the same room at the same time? Do we have that many math teachers? The headaches of the school administrator and students are soothed with the aid of a microcomputer.

- The library's card catalogue is much more easily updated and researched with a microcomputer. Looking for a particular topic? No need to fumble through dusty drawers full of cards. Just type the subject into the terminal and receive a printed list of books to check out. Who has that library book? When is it due back? How many books were not returned last year? How many books were added last year? The school administrator has access to information needed for library planning.

- Student records kept on a microcomputer are easily updated and retrieved in seconds. How many seniors will we have next year? What was the failure rate for each teacher? Does Alfred have enough credits to graduate? Should a notice about absenteeism be sent to Carol's parents? What will we show on our equal opportunity report?

- The three r's can be drilled on microcomputers. Reading, spelling, writing, and arithmetic lend themselves well to computer instruction.

- Illustrating almost any concept can be done with computer graphics or simulation. They say a picture is worth a thousand words.

- Eye-hand coordination, rapid reaction time, and other manual skills can be practiced on a microcomputer by playing games. A little target practice with photon torpedoes and Klingon ships will sharpen anyone's response.

Microcomputers are used by educators to improve proficiency levels by performing drill and practice, providing basic information, illustrating concepts, using simulated activities, performing experiments, demonstrating social phenomena, interacting with the student, providing immediate feedback, motivating the student, and relieving educators from student management tasks.

Microcomputers will play an increasingly more important role in the education of youngsters and adults. It's up to the educators and trainers to become "literate" in the field to insure the best application of this important training tool.

4

---

101 BUSINESS APPLICATIONS

An entire book could be written about the many business applications for microcomputers. Published software is becoming more common and affordable, thus further expanding the possibilities every day. The hobbiest-business users are inventing specialized programs which adapt the microcomputer to highly specific tasks.

ARCHITECTS USE MICROS FOR ENERGY ANALYSIS

Economic and ecological pressures and tax incentives pressure architects and builders to design and construct energy-efficient buildings and homes. The microcomputer allows the architect to construct a model at a much lower cost.

Insulation properties, glass conductivity, size and number of windows, compass orientation, weather information, natural shading, and many other factors are entered into the thermal modeling equation. The architect varies the factors, for example compass orientation, and determines the energy efficiency effects on the computer simulated model home.

These techniques are particularly valuable in designing homes or buildings using passive solar energy. The heat storage capacity of materials, glazing, etc. and the heat-loss rate are added to the equation for evaluation. In this way the architect can match the appropriate construction materials to the structure.

The best combination of factors is determined in minutes and with no construction costs.

DIETITIANS AND NUTRITIONISTS BALANCE DIETS

Many people need to eat special diets to control weight or medical problems such as diabetes and cardiovascular occlusion. People on kosher, vegetarian, and health food diets also must pay particular attention to the balance of foods they eat to insure proper nutrition. Dietitians and nutritionists can design diets and menus with the aid of a microcomputer in a fraction of the time previously required.

Hundreds of foods are entered into the computer, indicating for each the amount of calories, salt, cholesterol, vitamins, protein, carbohydrates, minerals, etc. A diet low in salt or high in protein is designed and tested to ensure that the recommended daily allowance of essential nutrients is met.

By adding information about height, weight, age, sex, and physical activity, a diet can be custom-designed to fulfill a particular individual's needs.

Cafeterias, hospitals, food services, and home dieters are using these systems to aid meal planning.

PERSONNEL PROBLEMS SOLVED

While mainframe (large) computers have relieved personnel professionals from the drudgery of paperwork, they remain unresponsive to immediate needs. Having to wait days or even weeks for reports or working with reports a month out of date proves to be cumbersome and sometimes embarrassing.

Now the microcomputer can do many of the daily tasks which personnel professionals need.

Personnel budgets. If a manager wants a list of all employees by location, hours worked, days worked, department, classification, or any other category, the microcomputer can produce a written report in minutes. Salary level, date of last salary review, performance rating, number of years on the job, etc. give the manager important information for making budget decisions.

Christmas, birthdays, promotions, new hires. Often the company newsletter highlights important events such as birthdays and promotions. Also, a Christmas party invitation list may be needed to address personalized letters. The microcomputer can provide instant information on personnel actions.

Salary reviews. A monthly listing of current salary reviews serves as a reminder to the supervisor or manager. Performance appraisals and salary actions can be monitored by personnel to insure changes within policy.

Benefits reporting. A summary of benefits allows the company to analyze expenses and to monitor the employee's use of optional programs.

Skill profiles. Often jobs can be filled with current employees if there is a way to locate who has the appropriate skills. A skill bank, when searched, provides a list of possible candidates. Also, the skill bank can highlight deficiencies in skill levels so the company can plan training programs.

EEO reports. The microcomputer can compile government and in-house reports which monitor equal employment opportunity compliance.

Employee statistics. Management often needs to know how the employees and departments rate in absenteeism, tardiness, turnover, and other performance factors. The microcomputer provides detailed reports to support management decisions and corrective actions.

Security. A listing of employees allowed on the premises after hours can be printed to give to the security guard for reference.

Word processing. All of the employment letters, the company newsletter, employment contracts, and other written documents are produced faster and with greater accuracy on a word processor. The microcomputer provides the flexibility of performing this service when equipped with a word processing printer.

Wage and salary survey statistics made easy. Collecting and analyzing salary survey data is time-consuming. Comparing survey information to employee data is difficult and requires many calculations and graphs. The microcomputer can relieve the drudgery and improve the accuracy of statistical studies. It can also recommend corrective actions to bring the company's pay practices more in line with the community.

RESERVATIONS CONFIRMED IN MINUTES

Companies can connect to national computer systems to make reservations for airlines, hotels, motels, and car rentals. An executive or sales representative can confirm travel plans with no mix-up or delay.

STOCK INFORMATION AND TRANSACTIONS WITH THE PUSH OF A BUTTON

Stock, commodity, and bond information is received and analyzed by the microcomputer. The information is compared to the executive's or company's portfolio, and recommendations are made to buy and sell. Graphic displays of stock performance and correlations to averages and other trends gives the stockholder information on which to base a decision. Telecommunications then allows the stockholder to communicate transactions to the broker.

ECONOMIC MODELING PROVIDES A LOOK INTO THE FUTURE

"What if" exercises allow managers to predict trends and to plan for catastrophe. Developing business plans in small organizations is often left for "dart board" exercises and shooting from the hip. With the microcomputer it's economically feasible for even a small firm to use sophisticated financial planning techniques.

Formulas and relationships are entered into the computer as "rules" of business. For example, if inflation increases 15 percent, the cost of materials will increase 15 percent. Or, if production increases 20 percent, the cost of labor will increase 10 percent. Once all of the relationships are entered, the manager can play "what if." For example, "What if inflation increases 10 percent, sales drop 10 percent, and advertising rates increase 8 percent? What should our advertising budget be?"

The microcomputer is useful for forecasting sales, developing business plans, and evaluating other business decisions that require a view into the future.

ROBOTS REPLACE WORKERS
IN HAZARDOUS AND REPETITIVE JOBS

They don't look like androids from science fiction lore, but micro-computer-controlled robots provide an improved quality of life for workers, reduce hazards, and improve quality control in many repetitive and dangerous jobs.

Many machine operations are computerized to save on set-up time and to improve tolerances.

AUTOMOBILE FUEL EFFICIENCY INCREASES

Automobile manufacturers use microprocessors to control electronic ignition and fuel/air mixture for carburetors. Emissions are controlled more efficiently and mileage improved.

TELECOMPUTING CONNECTS YOU
TO THE WORLD

The benefits we've gained thus far from telecomputing are like the tip of the iceberg. We haven't seen anything yet.

Instant flight information; stock transactions at your finger tips; market prices on commodities, livestock, and gold; weather information for farmers and solar heating installations; news around the world; a library to browse in; banking at home and at the office; and bill paying without checks; all this is possible in the near future.

With the microcomputer, satellites, telephone lines, and two-way cable television, a new world of communication lies ahead. Two-way communication, with the microcomputer acting as an intelligent terminal, allows the user to "talk" with mainframe computers anywhere in the world.

A PICTURE IS WORTH A THOUSAND WORDS

The slide presentation to top management is scheduled for 10 A.M. and you just found that inventory shrinkage was photographed at 40 percent instead of .40 percent. No time to have the artwork redone or the slide reshot. But there is time! With a microcomputer, the graphics can be called up like text in a word processor. The correction is made and the slide is reproduced in minutes.

Or better still, let the microcomputer project the slide onto a large screen television. Show the line on the graph climbing from year to year on earned profits. There's nothing like a little action to keep your audience awake. Need to update it next year? Just edit the "slide" stored in the computer's memory. No need for new artwork.

These are just a few advantages of computer graphics. The "slides" are up-to-date, faster to produce, and can show action or progression during the presentation. Also, simulations can demonstrate a machine operating, special effects can keep the audience alert and entertained, and the impact of computer graphics can change minds more rapidly.

Computer graphics are being used by companies in management presentations, by architects in designing buildings and homes, by interior decorators for design and layout; and by engineers to study mechanical designs.

Anywhere a picture makes the message or problem more clear, computer graphics may be the answer.

IT'S NOT WALT DISNEY

Animators use computer graphics to "draw" animation for the Saturday morning cartoons. Production is faster and less expensive than hand drawing.

GAMES ARE FOR PROFIT

Although we generally think of games as a home application for microcomputers, what is a game to you is profit to someone else. The computer game industry is one of the most lucrative applications for home computers.

Now computer games are available on cable television. Just plug in your computer at home and select from hundreds of games available from the satellite.

New York wants to send a contract to Los Angeles to be signed before 5 P.M. The word processor creates the document and the computer transmits the message via telephone lines to the microcomputer in Los Angeles. The Los Angeles computer prints out a perfect copy on the word processing printer only minutes after the message is sent. The deadline is met.

Because computers send messages much faster than any other way, the amount of long distance time (and money) spent is far less.

WEATHER PREDICTIONS

Meteorologists cannot create on a microcomputer the complex weather patterns that mainframes do, but they can isolate certain factors and study them for a limited geographical area. Also, the microcomputer weather simulation is easier for students to grasp.

THOSE BEAUTIFUL PICTURES FROM SATURN

Computer-enhanced photographs made the pictures from our space probes sharp and clear. Microcomputers are being used on earth to analyze pictures of license plates on speeding automobiles and to clarify films of burglars robbing banks. Identification is more certain with the aid of the microcomputer.

GEARS, PULLEYS, LEVERS . . .
WILL IT WORK?

Engineers use microcomputers to design chemical processing plants, to assess stress in high-rise structures, and to simulate mechanical operating conditions.

The microcomputer is to engineering design what the wind tunnel is to aerodynamic research. Simulations allow the experimenter to try different ideas without damage to equipment or expensive model making.

MUSIC TO MY EARS

Microcomputers assist musicians in composition and "editing" much like the word processor does for the author. As an added bonus, the microcomputer can be plugged into a music synthesizer and the composer can hear the results immediately.

NO MORE DEAD FROGS

Biologists are using microcomputers to analyze data, to predict results through simulation, to produce three-dimensional graphics of microbes seen in two dimensions, to monitor experiments over 24-hour periods, and to control environmental conditions such as temperature and humidity.

FITTING HUMANS TO MACHINES

Actually, it's the reverse: fitting machines to humans. The design of a lawnmower handle or the contour of a bucket seat can be engineered to insure optimal use, wear, and comfort for the consumer.

These designs become even more critical when safety is considered. For example, how should an automobile windshield be designed for the best visibility and minimum glare? How can a 50-ton press be disabled if the operator's hands are in the way? Microcomputers are providing the answers in design and control systems.

Other issues that microcomputers are addressing include productivity and efficiency. What are the most efficient arm motions to retrieve and assemble parts? When should quality control check production to avoid excessive production costs? How often should employees take breaks to maximize productivity?

Equipment design and operation must "fit" human characteristics if they are to work together safely and efficiently. Microcomputers are helping engineers and managers to bridge the gap.

WHEN WILL IT BREAK?

Scientists and engineers need to know the properties of materials used to construct buildings, roads, bridges, airplane wings, and other structures. Microcomputers are used to monitor test results and perform statistical analysis.

Simulations allow scientists to predict the behavior of materials under various environmental conditions such as subfreezing weather or high winds.

INVESTORS' DELIGHT

Many people hesitate to invest their hard-earned money because they would have to trust a broker or financial manager to optimize their earnings. Or, they would have to analyze all of those charts, trends, histories, and volumes of daily data to make financial decisions.

The microcomputer has the answer. It will do the work with you. Price watching, technical analysis, fundamental analysis, and portfolio monitoring is brought right into your office. The microcomputer will also act as your secretary to compose correspondence telling your broker what actions to take on your behalf.

CONTROL THE COMPANY FROM YOUR CHAIR

Well, not quite, but almost. Microcomputers are being increasingly used in control functions.

Laboratories use them to monitor test results and environmental conditions. The computer can adjust the thermostat or humidifier to maintain controlled conditions.

Typesetters no longer wear green-shaded caps. Instead, they type in and edit the copy on a microcomputer. Engraving, printing, calligraphy, and writing on parchment can all be controlled with a microcomputer.

Lasers used to cut and weld are controlled with microcomputers. The movable table or cart carrying the materials is positioned precisely by the microcomputer so that the laser cuts it with microscopic accuracy.

Office buildings and hotels control heating and air-conditioning systems by computer to maximize comfort and reduce utility bills.

44

Sensors throughout the building tell the microcomputer when to turn the heat on and off.

IRS, WATCH OUT!

Tired of doing taxes? Of remembering all of those instructions and rules? No problem for the microcomputer. Just enter your financial data and it will crank out the answers.

Should you make a charitable contribution on December 31? Calculate in minutes the effect on your taxes. Now you can make intelligent decisions to manage your finances.

ADDRESS 5,000 ENVELOPES

Need 5,000 envelopes addressed and sorted by zip code for bulk mail? The microcomputer can do it. Not only can it reproduce the list as needed in the future, but the list can be edited to change addresses or to delete dead files.

A doctor changes his address and wants to notify his patients; a lawn mower shop has a spring tune-up special for customers; an advertiser wants to reach all heads of household in a geographical area—the microcomputer provides quick, accurate, and uncomplaining service to the business operator.

PERSONALIZE THE LETTER TOO?

Merging the mailing list with the text of a letter to produce personalized letters is also done by microcomputers. The computer can even imbed the person's first name in the body of the letter, "As you know, Bob, we appreciate your business and hope..." When typed on a word processing printer, the customer will never know the difference.

WHERE'S THAT FILE?

Information! Information! Information! But how can it be located, sorted, organized, and edited with ease? Answer, the microcomputer.

What's the inventory level for part number 2381? Is Mrs. Brown's videotape recorder repaired? How many kites did the XYZ Discount Store order each year for the past five years? What medicines is Mr. Kilpatrick taking? What is the credit limit for ABC Supply? What accounts receivable are 90 days past due? How many orders did we get last year for model XR80 dishwashers? The list goes on and on.

Managers have great needs to monitor inventory levels, client and customer status, product sales, records, and financial accounts. The microcomputer provides information and reports to managers and business owners in a timely, meaningful, and accurate fashion.

GENERAL LEDGER AND FINANCIAL RECORD KEEPING

Keeping an accurate, balanced set of books can be boring and a hassle to many business owners. Now the microcomputer can relieve much of the drudgery.

Checks written and invoices received are entered into the computer and coded by account numbers. The computer can write checks to pay the bills, create invoices to send to customers, alert the manager of past due accounts, project cash flow needs into the future, compute the payroll, and create a general ledger.

Balance Sheets and Statements of Profits are generated as needed to monitor the business's performance.

SHOULD YOU PAY OFF THAT LOAN?

Loan programs tell you what effect paying off a loan early will have to the total expense. Even the effects of inflation can be considered in calculations. Sometimes increasing payments by only $10 per month can save thousands of interest dollars on long-term loans.

IS IT A GOOD RETURN ON INVESTMENT?

The microcomputer can compute earnings on savings deposits and certificates of deposit. Is the IRA fund the best place to put your earnings? What will be the future balance in an account given regular deposits? Now you can calculate the best plan for investing your money.

INVENTORY CONTROL IS PROFIT CONTROL

Controlling inventory of repair parts, merchandise, or raw materials controls liquidity. If cash for paying bills is tied up in excessive, slow-moving inventory, creditors go begging. If inventory doesn't turn over, the return on investment diminishes.

Microcomputers give fast information to the manager on when to order, how much to order, what price to charge, what's back-ordered, which vendor to use, as well as a history for an item's movement.

The manager can plan future purchases, parts returns, and manufacturing schedules with reports from the microcomputer.

STREAMLINE PRODUCTION

Microcomputers are used to control raw material purchases and thus avoid expensive overbuying and shortages that bog down production. Computer-generated production time estimates facilitate scheduling, cost accounting, and estimating manpower requirements.

Material requirements planning and production planning become manageable with a microcomputer.

WHERE DOES IT ALL STOP?

Not with these 101 business applications. We've only scratched the surface. It's hard to believe that microcomputers only became popular during the late 1970s. Ten years from now we probably won't believe the limitations of our imagination.

5

CENTRAL FILES:
THE DATA BASE
MANAGEMENT
CONCEPT

Many company record systems are organized so that file duplication is common. The Accounting Department has an Accounts Receivable file on customers receiving goods. The Marketing Department has a file on customers which rates their worth. The Credit Department has a file on customers to determine their credit line. And so it goes.

"Why do we have all of these separate files?" the marketing executive asked. "Every time there's a change, it has to be communicated and posted to all of these different departments. Why not have one central file which everyone can use?"

That question began the thinking now known as *data base*. It wasn't as easily to implement as it might appear, because the needs of the different departments varied. The Accounts Receivable Department didn't need the same information as Marketing, and Credit needed yet something else. The task of creating the central file or data base required

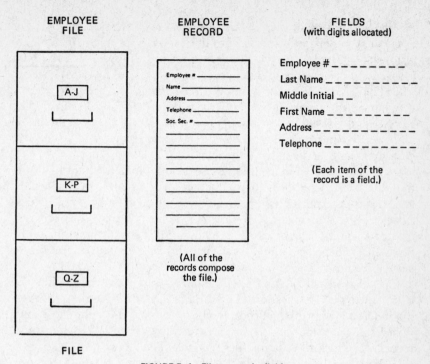

EMPLOYEE FILE	EMPLOYEE RECORD	FIELDS (with digits allocated)

EMPLOYEE FILE

A-J

K-P

Q-Z

FILE

EMPLOYEE RECORD

Employee # _____
Name _____
Address _____
Telephone _____
Soc. Sec. # _____

(All of the records compose the file.)

FIELDS (with digits allocated)

Employee # _ _ _ _ _ _ _ _

Last Name _ _ _ _ _ _ _ _ _ _

Middle Initial _ _

First Name _ _ _ _ _ _ _ _ _

Address _ _ _ _ _ _ _ _ _ _

Telephone _ _ _ _ _ _ _ _ _ _

(Each item of the record is a field.)

FIGURE 5–1. Files, records, fields.

finding out *all* of the information the company needed to know about a customer.

The factors such as name, address, zip code, telephone number, credit rating, annual dollar volume, etc. are called *fields*. All of the fields for one customer are called a *record*. The collection of records for the customer file forms the *data base file*.

So, a *microcomputer data base* is a large file of organized data which all users draw upon for a common pool of up-to-date information.

The *Data Base Management System* (DBMS) is the software system for designing, setting up, and subsequently managing a data base. It allows the programmer to specify which data needs to be stored, and can strip off sorted reports from the data base. For example, if the Marketing Department wanted a list of customers by zip code, the DBMS would sort the file by zip code and print out the report. If the Credit Department wanted a list of customers sorted by size of credit line, the DBMS would sort the file by that field and write the report.

The DBMS is not a processing or transaction driven system. It performs only simple calculations, for example totals and subtotals, and the data is not automatically updated as other systems change. For example, the percent of credit line utilized will not fluctuate as transactions are posted to receivables and order processing. Therefore, on a microcomputer, data base is not good for inventory or financial systems.

The DBMS will create, sort, edit, add, change, and delete records. A new customer can be added to the data base. The DBMS will sort the customer file by any field. The fields can be edited to adjust the information. New information can be added to the record, and an inactive customer can be deleted from the data base.

The other programs in the system can call upon the information in the data base to perform their functions. For example, a mailing list generation program pulls information out of the data base on the customer's name and address. A customer performance analysis program extracts various pieces of information describing the customer including fields like type of business, location, sales representative, number of years in business, and annual sales.

By having all of the customer information in a central file, the company avoids duplication of creating and updating customer information and insures that all company functions are using the same data. Other data bases that companies use are employee skills files, personnel records, product information files, and telephone lists.

Most microcomputers do not have enough memory to accommodate large data base files. However, as business applications increase and computer memory (storage) becomes less expensive, data base management will play an increasingly important role in microcomputer applications.

GLOSSARY

Data Base. A large file of organized data which all users draw upon for a common pool of up-to-date information.

Data Base File. A collection of records which form a data base.

DBMS (Data Base Management System). The software system for designing, creating, and subsequently managing a data base, e.g., creating files, editing files, and sorting files.

Fields. The individual factors in a record such as name, address, zip code, telephone number, and date of birth.

Record. A collection of fields forming one unit of data, e.g., an employee record.

6

DEATH OF THE TYPEWRITER: THE WORD PROCESSOR

The prospect of having to edit and retype material composed on a typewriter is unbearable after only a few months of using a microcomputer word processing system.

Anyone who's been "spoiled" by the processed word finds that using a typewriter is equivalent to using stone axes to chop wood. However, selecting a word processing system is not an easy task.

The first decision to be made is whether to buy a *dedicated word processor* which will only do word processing or whether to buy a microcomputer and a word processing software package. Even more difficult is evaluating the efficiency and ease with which the word processing system operates. The features and benefits of each vary considerably; however, there are a number of key items to examine.

DEDICATED WORD PROCESSORS
ARE CUSTOMIZED

Attorneys, realtors, writers, secretaries, and numerous professionals who generate letters, reports, contracts, and large volumes of writing are turning to dedicated word processors (wp's) to improve efficiency and quality. As a bonus, much of the drudgery of final production is removed from the typist's duties.

Because dedicated wp's are designed for a narrow application, the programmers, engineers, and manufacturers can tailor the equipment, software, and manuals for the word processing user. The ease of learning and operating the dedicated wp makes these systems attractive to office applications.

Dedicated wp's have upper- and lower-case letter capabilities, have at least an 80-character width, a high resolution screen, special control keys to perform complex text-editing functions, and a letter-quality printer.

The user commands the word processor to display the text on the screen (CRT = *Cathode Ray Tube*) in the format in which it will appear on the printed page. This permits format editing so that the final copy conforms to the typist's design. The high resolution screen is easy to read and not visually tiring. Special keys allow the user to move text, save text, merge text, and insert text with a single stroke. The dedicated wp has definite advantages over the microcomputer in rapid, high-volume word processing applications.

The dedicated wp is also more expensive than the microcomputer. The repair time tends to be faster and service contracts, though expensive, are available to repair it on-site. The wp lacks flexibility. However, if it is used constantly, a dedicated word processor more than pays for itself in efficient productivity.

MICROCOMPUTERS DO MUCH MORE

A business user, home computer user, or hobbiest who has moderate wp demands and who can use the other services a microcomputer provides should consider the microcomputer. The microcomputer tends to be less expensive even with the CRT and letter-quality wp *printer*. In addition, the computer has available for use *applications software* (programs with specific functions) such as Accounts Receivable, Payroll, Accounts Payable, Inventory Control, Information Retrieval, and games.

The wp applications program may not be as efficient or as *powerful* (versatile) as the dedicated system, but the versatility of the computer as a whole more than compensates for this minor inconvenience. In addition, the microcomputer can be reprogrammed to perform unusual wp functions while dedicated wp's do not have modifiable programs.

WHICH ONE IS BEST?

The question is not "Which one is best?" but "Which one meets my needs?" Where constant use, high wp production, fast repair service, and powerful editing capabilities are needed, the dedicated wp quickly justifies its higher price. If the user requires more versatility from a piece of equipment to justify the expense, a microcomputer is usually the better buy.

NOT ALL WP'S WORK THE SAME

There are more variations of wp systems than there are types of equipment. Again, the fanciest or most expensive wp program may not be the "best" for a particular application. Each wp function should be weighed against the needs of the user. Whether a microcomputer with a word processor package or a dedicated word processor is purchased, the following options should be considered:

Upper and lower case. The printer and the screen should be capable of displaying upper- and lower-case letters. Some screens print all letters in upper case and highlight with a white square the capitalized letters. Upper-case text is difficult to read; therefore, this is not a good system for volume production.

Special characters. An application may require special characters such as engineering and mathematical symbols. The keyboard, CRT, program, and printer should be capable of producing these characters.

Ten-key pad. Where numerical entry is frequent, a ten-key pad improves efficiency and accuracy.

Screen load. The screen load is the amount of text the CRT (or black and white television screen) is capable of displaying at one time. Screen load is measured in characters per line and lines per screen. The larger the screen load the better able the user is to perform format editing. Usually 2–3 loads is equal to one printed page, single-spaced.

Scrolling. Page scrolling is the ability to print the text line-by-line or page-by-page on the screen. It is particularly useful for proofreading and editing.

Wrap around. This feature permits the user to type continuously without striking the *return* key at the end of the line. The wp formats the text automatically at the time it is displayed on the screen or on the printer.

Split screen. The ability to see one part of the text while editing another part on the screen. This helps in writing parallel construction and moving text.

Cursor control. This is the ability to position your pen, so to speak. The *cursor* is a highlighted mark, usually a bright square on the screen. The next entry on the keyboard is recorded where the cursor is positioned on the screen. The ability to position the cursor is critical to efficiency. The cursor should move from right to left, left to right, up, and down without affecting the text. Some systems only allow the cursor to move one space or line at a time, while others allow the rapid movement from one position to another. Special commands are available to "go" (move the pen) to the beginning of the text, to the end of the text, or to a special word in the text. The power of the cursor control function is directly related to the power of the wp system.

Page oriented. A page-oriented system allows the cursor to jump to any desired page.

Line oriented. A line-oriented system allows the cursor to move anywhere on the screen. Single lines can be displayed and edited.

Mode control. The number of mode controls also determines how efficiently a system operates. Some systems require that the user select *write* (add text), *edit* (change text), or *jump around* (move cursor) before commanding that operation. Other programs allow all of these functions to occur at once without special instructions for mode selection. Dedicated wp's tend to have fewer control commands to perform complex functions than microcomputers, although this isn't always true.

Screen formating. This capability allows the user to visualize the printed format on the screen. Margins can be adjusted to different line widths, page length can be specified, titles are centered, etc.

Printer formating. This capability allows the user to control the printer for line spacing (single, double, etc.), line width, page length, top and bottom margins, right and left margin justification, proportional spacing, and pausing. Some systems allow the entry of additional text directly from the keyboard after a "pause" command. This permits personalization of a letter, for example.

Auto "normal" formating. This enters standard format commands when the system is *power up* (turned on).

Flush right. The right margin is justified.

Centering. This is especially useful for titles.

Vertical centering. The system locates the text on the page evenly from top to bottom.

Tabs (indenting). The beginning of a line is placed at a selected tab. Useful for outlines and reports.

Auto indenting. Every line is placed at a manually preselected tab.

Paragraph indenting. Indents each new paragraph (only the first line).

Local editing. The system is capable of inserting and deleting characters and words as well as dropping or adding lines, paragraphs, and pages.

Strikeover. If a character is struck with the cursor positioned over another character on the screen, the original character is "erased" and the new character entered.

Replace editing. The ability to edit a specific word or phrase throughout the text with a single command. For example, if the user wants to change the word "paper" to "document" everywhere in the text, a single command will accomplish the task. This is especially useful if a word is misspelled in a letter. The incorrect spelling can be corrected throughout the text with little effort.

Search (Find). The ability of the system to locate every occurence of a word or group of characters in the text. For example, the user might want to *find* "paper" to manually change it to "document" in some instances. The wp will present each occurence and allow the user to manually enter the change if desired. This capability is especially useful in creating an index.

Delete editing. The ability to delete (erase) a specific word or phrase throughout the text with a single command. For example, if the user wants to remove every occurence of the word "Mr.", a single command will accomplish the task.

Global editing. The abilities to search, find, delete, and replace text (see *Delete editing*).

Blocks. The ability of a wp to identify a section of text for the purpose of deleting, moving, or duplicating it. This gives the wp the ability to cut and paste the text. "Blocks" of text can be moved to other locations, deleted, or duplicated (transferred).

Merge. This ability allows the user to combine two pieces of information from different files. For example, if personalized letters are required in large volume, a mailing list with names and addresses can be combined with the text of the letter to create personalized letters. Even the reference to the person's name can be entered in the body of the letter. Also, some applications require repeated use of specific paragraphs as in legal contracts. These paragraphs can be stored in another file and pulled into the document as needed.

Glossary. Another term for *merge,* where commonly used names, sentences, or paragraphs can be pulled into the text from other files.

Dictionary. Some wp's (mostly dedicated) have the ability to check the user's spelling. The misspelled word is highlighted so the alerted user can correct the mistake. Up to 50,000 words are available as well as the capability to create a customized dictionary of 10,000 additional words.

Chaining. Normally when a new file is loaded in the computer or wp, the previous file is erased. Chaining allows the user to stack one file on top of another, that is, to build a long piece of text from smaller pieces in separate files. Some wp's call this merging files.

Directories/Menus. The wp has the ability to create a file index on the *floppy disk* (storage medium for text—the electronic filing cabinet). This index tells the user what is located on the disk and where. Some systems allow the display of the directory while entering text and others require that the text be saved (stored on the disk) prior to seeing the directory. Those who forget to save the text on the latter system are sadly surprised after looking at the directory to find that their last entries have been erased forever.

Embedded commands. Formating commands (codes) which instruct the CRT and printer how to display the text, e.g., centering, tabs, new line, paragraph, line spacing, margins, go to top of next page (top of form), and pause. Some wp's allow commands to the printer to vary during the printing operation.

Headers/footers. The ability to "slug" each page with the title or some identifying message at the top or bottom.

Pagination. The automatic numbering of printed pages. Some wp's allow specification of the placement of the number on the page and others put it in a standard place. The series of numbers can begin at a specific starting point, for example a book chapter might begin on page 15, so the first page printed would be labeled "15."

Hyphenation. To make the text as attractive as possible, some wp's tell the user which words should be hyphenated and allow the user to designate the breaking point. The rules for hyphenation are so complex, it is almost impossible to have a program accurately hyphenate.

Print modes. This allows the user to command the printer to print continuously to the end of the document, to stop after each page (this allows insertion of stationery), or to stop within the page so text may be added from the keyboard.

Subscript/Superscript. Some mathematical or chemistry equations require half-line spacing, for example to indicate a number is squared. The printer, also, must have the capability of producing the printed character.

Underlining/Boldface printing. This print command is only useful if the printer can backspace (to underline) or can produce the boldface quality.

Mathematical calculations. Some applications require the totaling of columns of figures. Simple mathematical functions can be performed and the results automatically entered to the text.

Invisible lines. Occasionally the author may want a "private" note inserted into the text, for example a reminder or indexing code. This text will not be printed.

Decimal alignment. The ability of the wp to line up the decimal points on calculations and figures entered. This is especially useful for billing and creating monthly reports.

DEFINE YOUR REQUIREMENTS

All of these functions sound fantastic. Many of them are expensive, especially if the program can perform them all. The user must identify which of these features are required and which are useful for the application. Also, the chosen options must be compatible with the equipment the wp program will run on.

Another consideration should be the operator's ability and training. Most applications require repeated use of only 10 to 15 of these functions. The others are seldom required. The operator frequently learns the commonly used processes and the rest go to waste.

OTHER CONSIDERATIONS

Whether the user purchases a dedicated system or a microcomputer, additional support is needed for the system. Procedures for file security, maintenance and service, catastrophe planning, physical file storage, machine access, documentation and file naming conventions and controls, work priority and scheduling, training and retraining, and back-up must be planned.

There are additional costs for installation and site preparation, start up inefficiency and support, special paper and ribbons, archive storage, communication (lines to other locations), special furniture, environmental control, carpet static protection, and upgrading when a new feature or program update is available. Not all of these are problems for every system, but the purchaser should inquire about and plan for them if they apply.

Above all, the people who use the word processor must like it. If they don't, the equipment will sit idle.

A word processing system makes duplicates of originals in minutes, produces perfect copies rapidly, reduces the need for proofreading, improves quality, reduces drudgery, increases productivity, and improves the user's quality of life. It's little wonder that someone spoiled with a word processor feels handicapped on a typewriter.

HOW TO SELECT
MICROCOMPUTER
HARDWARE

7

THE LIMITS OF
INTERNAL MEMORY

A microcomputer has limited space to store instructions and data. A typical breakdown for a microcomputer with 64 memory units (*kilobytes*), would be:

  2 units for operating the monitor (screen)
  30 units for instructions on what to do
  10–15 units on understanding the language telling it what to do
  20 or so units left to store the data to manipulate (usable storage/memory)

Even though 64 kilobytes (65,536 characters or numbers) sounds like a large memory capacity, the usable storage may only be 20 units or 20,480 characters. (1 *byte* = 1 character; 1,024 *bytes* = 1 *kilobyte* = 1K).

The allocation of memory varies according to the system, the brand of computer, and the hardware used. However, all microcomputers have definite *internal memory* limitations.

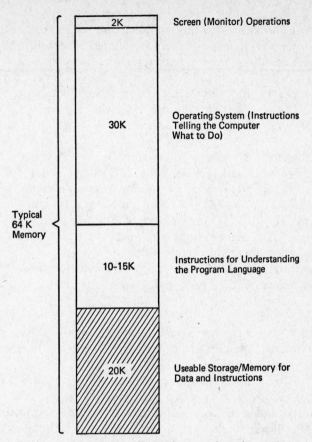

2K	Screen (Monitor) Operations
30K	Operating System (Instructions Telling the Computer What to Do)
10-15K	Instructions for Understanding the Program Language
20K	Useable Storage/Memory for Data and Instructions

Typical 64 K Memory

FIGURE 7–1. The allocation of internal memory in a microcomputer.

COMMON TYPES OF INTERNAL MEMORY

The inside of the computer contains *chips* (semiconductors) that store information. These electronic components are responsible for revolutionizing the computer industry by reducing the size of a computer from room-size to the size of a cigar box. A chip 1/10 of a square inch can store 4,000 *bits* of information (8 *bits* = 1 byte = 1 character).

Read-Only Memory   Some *chips* in the microcomputer are prerecorded with information and data. After the chips are manufactured, instructions are burned into them. Once burned, the chips hold their memory contents and will not accept any modifications. Since these chips can only be read and not written (altered by the user), they are called *Read-Only Memory Chips* (ROM). They are dedicated to essential functions, cannot be altered or erased, and are not destroyed by turning the computer off. ROM contains the programs used repeatedly by the computer. For example, ROM may contain the operating system that tells the computer how to communicate with the *peripherals* (devices attached such as a disk drive unit or printer).

Random-Access Memory   Other chips in the computer's memory are able to receive information for temporary storage. RAM chips (the 20 kilobytes of usable memory left in the above example) can be randomly *accessed* and thus are called *Random-Access Memory*. In a few millionths of a second, the CPU can locate a piece of information in RAM.

The time it takes the computer to read information from a memory location is called the memory *access time.*

The contents of RAM are lost when the electrical power is turned off. Power failures and surges wreak havoc with RAM and the microcomputer operator.

Ideally, the computer would have as much RAM as possible. However, internal memory (RAM and ROM) is a relatively expensive form of information storage.

When the computer is first turned on, RAM contains nothing of meaning. As ROM is powered up the computer "knows" how to go to the disk drive and load RAM with programs and data from the floppy disk. RAM is filled with the application programs and the system begins. This is commonly referred to as *booting* the system.

The average user doesn't need to know much more about internal memory than what has been discussed to this point. Most readers will want to skip from here to the next chapter which covers secondary memory (floppy disks, cassette tapes, and hard disks). The more serious user, however, may wish to continue with this chapter to dissect the electronic workings more completely.

FURTHER DISSECTION OF INTERNAL MEMORY

Besides ROM chips and RAM chips there are a number of other electronic memory components inside the "black box." PROM (Programmable Read-Only Memory) is a type of read-only memory which can be programmed by the user with a PROM Burner. The PROM is purchased empty of information and is programmed by the user with a PROM Burner which puts the bit patterns into the chip.

EPROM (Erasable Programmable Read-Only Memory) is a PROM which can be erased and reprogrammed. It sounds somewhat like RAM, but an EPROM can only be erased with a device using ultraviolet light. EPROMs cannot be written over like RAM and they will not lose their programming when the computer is powered down. A *PROM Burner* is used to reprogram the EPROM.

The *Piggyback EPROM* is a developmental tool. The Piggyback EPROM is attached physically to ROM and programmed and debugged until the desired performance is achieved. Then it is converted into a ROM chip for permanent storage of the information.

All of these memory devices are *nonvolatile* in that they retain their memory when power is lost. Another term for this information is *firmware* since it is neither *software* or *hardware* but is a combination of both.

Internal memory is also used as a *buffer*. Different parts of the computer system work at different rates. For example, the printer may operate at 45 characters (bytes) per second while the CPU is sending out data thousands of times faster. If there is a place for the information to go until the printer is capable of accepting it, the CPU can go on to other activities while the printer is operating. The buffer provides a halfway house where the information is stored temporarily and thus serves to cushion the impact of the different speeds at which different parts of a computer handle data.

NEW TECHNOLOGY

New technology on the horizon promises larger memory capacity for less money. *Bubble Memory* is not commercially available, yet the term surfaces frequently. This new magnetic technology is faster and more reliable than disk storage.

Another promising development in memory technology is CCD (Charge-Coupled Device). Though still expensive and rare, it promises to provide new horizons in mass-produced, low-cost memory devices.

SUMMARY

The three types of memory are ROM, RAM, and auxilliary. ROM is the working memory containing the instructions for doing repetitive tasks and for communicating with *peripheral devices* (secondary storage devices, monitor, keyboard, etc.). ROM is valuable because it is available immediately when the computer is turned on. RAM contains the detailed instructions and data input from external memory or the keyboard. RAM is erased when the computer is turned off. Long-term memory is stored on tapes, floppy disks, and hard disks. Very large quantities of information are thus available to the computer but not as quickly as with main memory.

Main Memory contains ROM, RAM, and their derivations. Internal memory consists of electrical circuits within the computer that allow the microcomputer to retain information. The CPU reads fastest from internal memory, but it is very expensive and thus limited. External storage in the form of tapes and disks expand the effective working memory of the microcomputer. To utilize the information in secondary storage, the data must be loaded into internal memory first.

GLOSSARY

Access Time. The time it takes for the computer to read information.

Bit. The smallest unit of memory in a microcomputer.

Boot. A set of instructions in ROM which are initiated by a manual switch. The instructions tell the computer what to do to start up the equipment.

Bubble Memory. A new technology that promises memory with larger capacity for less money.

Buffer. A block of memory where the CPU can temporarily put information so that another piece of equipment which works at a different speed can find it when it needs the information.

Byte. A unit of measure equal to the amount of information needed to describe one letter, number, or character.

Cassette Tape. A tape similar to a music recording tape which is used to store large volumes of information in sequential order. A secondary storage medium for a microcomputer.

CCD (Charge-Coupled Device). A new type of memory which, when mass-produced, may bring the price of internal storage down.

Chip. An electronic component of a microcomputer.

CPU (Central Processing Unit). The "brain" of the microcomputer that performs the arithmetic and logic functions. The CPU controls all computer functions, sends commands to the peripheral devices, and controls access to memory.

Disk Drive Unit. The peripheral device that spins a floppy or hard disk and reads information from and writes information to the disk storage media.

EPROM (Erasable Programmable Read-Only Memory). A PROM which can be erased and reprogrammed with special devices.

Floppy Disk. A thin, mylar, record-shaped disk housed in a protective jacket. The magnetic surface stores large amounts of information for microcomputer use.

Handshaking. The signals or pulses that establish synchonization between the disk drive (or other devices) and the computer.

Hard Disk. A metallic, record-shaped disk, usually hermetically sealed from the environment. The magnetic surface can store large amounts of information for microcomputer use.

Interface Controller and Formater. The electronic device that interfaces signals that control the position of the read/write head, that formats the data on the disk, and implements handshake routines (programs).

Internal Memory. The electrical circuits within the computer that allow the microcomputer to retain information. Internal memory consists of ROM and RAM.

K. Abbreviation for kilobyte.

Kilobyte. 1,024 bytes of information (characters).

Load. To transfer information into the computer or onto a secondary storage medium.

Main Memory. ROM, RAM, and their derivations. See *Internal Memory.*

Medium. A secondary storage magnetic surface, e.g. tape, floppy disk, and hard disk.

Memory. The circuits or devices that store information for the computer to use.

Nonvolatile. A type of memory chip which retains its memory when power is turned off, e.g., ROM and PROM.

Peripheral. An input or output device attached to a microcomputer, e.g., keyboard, disk drive, monitor.

Piggyback EPROM. A developmental tool used to design ROM chips.

Positioner. The arm in the floppy disk drive that moves the read/write head to the proper track on the disk.

PROM (Programmable Read-Only Memory). A type of read-only memory (ROM) which can be programmed by the user.

PROM Burner. A special device used to program a PROM or reprogram an EPROM.

RAM (Random-Access Memory). Chips in the computer that can randomly transfer information to and from the CPU. The scratch pad for the CPU where temporary information is stored. RAM is alterable and the information in RAM is erased when the computer is turned off.

Read/Write Head. The component of the disk drive that transfers information to and from the disk. Its function is similar to that of a needle on a record player.

Removable Cartridge. A type of hard disk that allows the use of multiple disks.

ROM (Read-Only Memory). Chips in the computer that are preprogrammed with the basic repetitive instructions to operate the computer. ROM is permanent and not erasable.

Secondary Storage. The tape, floppy disk, and hard disk systems used by a microcomputer to store large amounts of information.

Track. Defined area on a disk where information is stored. Tracks are arranged in concentric circles on the disk.

8

SECONDARY STORAGE: "UNLIMITED" MEMORY

Since a microcomputer can only store a limited amount of information at one time, it is necessary to use only a few applications simultaneously. For example, an Inventory System with thousands of data entries will consume most of the computer's internal memory (Random-Access Memory). Therefore, it is necessary to remove the Inventory System to make room for other programs and data. Secondary storage media make this process possible.

Main Memory (Internal Memory = RAM and ROM) is expensive in relation to the amount of information it can store. External storage in the form of tapes and disks greatly expands the effective working memory of the microcomputer at a reduced expense.

The three types of secondary memory used with microcomputers are *cassette tapes, floppy disks,* and *hard disks.* Tapes hold over 1 million bytes (characters) and take 2–3 minutes to access. Floppy disks hold from 100 thousand to 3 million bytes and take ⅓ second to 2 seconds to access. Hard disks hold from 5 million to 100 million bytes and access in a thousandth of a second.

Secondary memory is the filing cabinet for the computer. The computer can search the *medium* (tape, floppy, hard disk) for specific data such as an inventory record. Or, the computer can receive (*load*) long lists of instructions (*programs*) from the medium. Data received from secondary storage is placed into the short-term working memory (RAM). The computer can manipulate or utilize the information stored in RAM very rapidly (millionths of a second access time). The results of the manipulations are transferred back (*loaded*) to secondary memory to be retained for future use. Back into the filing cabinet, so to speak.

CASSETTE TAPE STORAGE

The cassette tape recorder used for recording sound is similar to the device used for storing data for the microcomputer. Some of the frequency responses of high fidelity music recorders can actually cause interference for computers. Specially designed units are more reliable for microcomputer use.

Although the storage capacity of tape is high, the *access time* (time to read data from the storage medium) is slow. Even with fast forward and fast rewind controls, it takes several minutes for the tape to move to the location where the desired data record is stored. The main reason for the delay is that the data is stored sequentially on tapes. We listen to music sequentially, so cassette tapes work well. But with data, the computer must read all the way through to where the desired record is stored. Thus finding a particular part number in an inventory file takes time.

It's risky inserting data on a tape since controlling the position of the tape in an inexpensive recorder is not precise. Tapes should be used for simple applications, such as loading game programs. Tapes are primarily for holding programs, *backing up* (copying) data, and storing sequential data.

FLOPPY DISK STORAGE

A *floppy disk* resembles a 45 rpm record. Because it is thin, the disk is flexible, thus the term "floppy." The advantage of floppy disks over

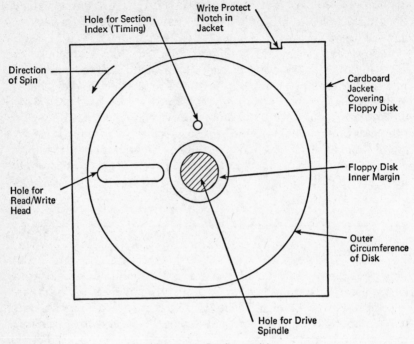

- Hole for Section Index (Timing)
- Write Protect Notch in Jacket
- Direction of Spin
- Cardboard Jacket Covering Floppy Disk
- Floppy Disk Inner Margin
- Hole for Read/Write Head
- Outer Circumference of Disk
- Hole for Drive Spindle

FIGURE 8–1 The floppy disk.

cassette tapes is that the *read/write head* (like a needle for a record player) can be positioned quickly anywhere on the disk. This reduces retrieval time and increases computer efficiency. The ability to pick up data anywhere on the disk is called *direct access*.

Each surface of the disk is covered with a magnetic iron oxide compound. The disk is sealed in a square cardboard holder to protect it from fingerprints and dirt. The inside of the jacket is covered with a low friction material that cleans the disk as it spins inside. The jacket and disk are inserted into the *disk drive unit*.

The jacket has several holes cut in it. A large center hole is used to install the disk on the drive unit. A slot in the jacket allows the read/write head to touch the disk. A small opening in the cardboard reveals a timing hole on the disk. A light shines through this hole and blinks on and off as the disk spins. The blinking light tells the computer where the disk is positioned and allows the computer to synchronize to its rotation. Another hole, if covered, protects the disk from being written on. This is similar to protecting a cassette tape from being recorded again.

Floppy disks come in two sizes. The 5¼ inch disk stores about 80,000 bytes (characters) and the 8 inch floppy stores up to 3 million bytes.

The *tracks* on the disk are not like the spiral grooves on a record. They are defined, concentric circles which are invisible to the eye.

Double density is a method for storing twice as much information on a floppy disk surface. *Dual sided double density* refers to the doubling of information on a disk side and using both sides of the disk for storage. By using these methods, over four times the information can be stored on a single disk.

At 300 rpm the opportunity for the read/write head to access the data on the disk is frequent. The *positioner* (the arm the head is mounted on) moves in and out to locate the head over the correct track called for by the computer.

The access time for floppy disk systems is ⅓ second to 2 seconds with most of that time spent moving the head to the appropriate track.

Because the head actually touches the disk surface, floppy disks will wear out. Losing 80 thousand characters of data or more is disasterous. It's important to keep a frequent back-up for emergencies.

The access speed of the floppy disk is limited by the rpm, the time required to move the positioner, and the density of the magnetic material on the mylar surface. Higher rpm physically distort the disk shape and ruin the data.

The hobbiest and the small business user usually use the reasonably priced floppy disk system. The storage capacity is adequate for most operations. More information can be made available by removing and inserting extra disks. The mechanism and controller for the disk drive unit is very sophisticated and surprisingly reliable.

HARD DISK STORAGE

The business user with large amounts of data, numerous applications, multiple terminals, and a greater need for reliability may find the hard disk system is the best device for secondary storage.

Hard disks are made of solid metal covered with a magnetic coating on one or both sides. The disk spins at very high speeds, stores between 5 million and 100 million bytes (characters) of information, and accesses within a thousandth of a second. The computer can read or write over 7 million bytes in a second with a hard disk.

The hard disk read/write head floats on a cushion of air not touching the hermetically sealed disk surface. As a result, the hard disk doesn't wear out like a floppy. Each track also has its own head, thus shortening the access time.

Removable cartridge hard disks allow the use of more than one disk. This system is expensive but provides flexibility. Less expensive hard disk systems contain an enclosed permanent disk.

A large amount of secondary storage is needed for storing and sorting large files, e.g., address labels and inventory. Storing large files on floppies may require the operator to remove and insert numerous disks. Frequent disk handling can cause mistakes and damage to the disks. Merging large files with floppies is nearly impossible because RAM will hold only small portions of information at any one time.

If two or more terminals are used, hard disks have a much shorter response time to user demands. As each terminal makes demands on the secondary storage, the user must wait in line, so to speak, to access the information. The longer it takes the drive to retrieve the information, and the more people making demands on the system, the longer the wait. The differences in hard and floppy disk access times becomes more and more noticeable as disk access demands increase.

Before deciding to purchase a hard disk system, the user should consider buying a second microcomputer with another floppy disk system. The price of two computers might be the same as adding one hard disk system. With two computers, though, the user has total back-up if the computer fails. If the one computer with a hard disk *goes down* (fails), the user is out of business until repair is made. The decision rests on the speed and volume of data required in a single file. Floppies cannot substitute for hard disks where large files must be manipulated or where rapid access is essential.

One business used their computer and two terminals for inventory control, customer files, and word processing. When the operating systems for every application were loaded into RAM, there was little internal memory left for creating new files. The business had to either go to a hard disk system with larger capacity and faster response time or purchase a second computer for word processing. The decision was made to purchase a second computer for word processing only.

PROTECTING THE INFORMATION: BACK-UP

All programs and stored data should be copied and safely stored in case of natural catastrophe or computer failure. *Back-up* (the copied information) may be on the same medium as the original data or may be stored on a less expensive medium. For example, floppy disks may be copied on tape and hard disks may be duplicated on floppies.

DISK OPERATING SYSTEM (DOS)

The *disk operating system* is the set of instructions which are needed by the computer to operate the disk drive. The DOS handles all input and output disk functions as well as head positioning. It also has instructions to save and load programs, that is to put information on the disk for storage or to take information off of the disk and put it in RAM.

The DOS makes demands on the computer of between 8 and 20 kilobytes of memory and may occupy up to 30 percent of the storage capacity of a floppy disk. A sophisticated DOS may make too great a demand on the microcomputer memory system.

For small microcomputers, it's better to have a simple DOS that uses less than 8K of RAM and minimal disk space.

SUMMARY

The three types of memory are main, long-term, and learned. Main memory (RAM and ROM) is the working memory containing the instructions for doing repetitive tasks and for communicating with *peripheral devices* (long-term storage devices, monitor, keyboard, etc.). The learned portion of main memory (RAM) contains the detailed instructions and data from secondary storage and keyboard entries.

Long-term memory is stored on tapes, floppy disks, and hard disks. Very large quantities of information are available to the computer but not as quickly as with main memory.

Cassette tapes are inexpensive and have a large capacity. They are primarily used as back-up for floppy disks since it is difficult to retrieve specific pieces of information from them.

Floppy disks provide relatively inexpensive, large capacity memory with quick access time. Since they are removable, multiple disks provide an infinite amount of information to the computer.

Hard disks are reliable, extremely fast, and have large storage capacities. They are best suited to applications requiring multiple terminals or where large amounts of data (files) must be manipulated.

The Disk Operating System (DOS) is the set of instructions which controls the operations of the disk drive secondary storage system. It should be simple since a complex DOS occupies too much memory for the small computer.

All programs and data files should be backed-up on another medium. Floppies are often used to back-up hard disks and other floppies. Tapes may also be used as back-up for either system. Without back-up, the user is extremely vulnerable to loss of information.

The amount of memory required by the user is determined by the applications and systems used on the computer. The dealer should be able to determine how much RAM the application requires and what the best secondary storage system is to satisfy the buyer's needs.

GLOSSARY

Access time. The time it takes for the computer to read information from a memory location, disk drive, or tape unit.

Back-up. The storage of information on an extra secondary storage medium for protection against physical damage or electrical distortion.

Byte. A unit of measure equal to enough information to describe one letter, number, or character.

Cassette Tape. A tape similar to a music recording tape used to store large volumes of information in sequential order. A secondary storage medium for a microcomputer.

CPU (Central Processing Unit). The "brain" of the microcomputer that performs the arithmetic and logic functions. The CPU controls all computer functions, sends commands to the peripheral devices, and controls access to memory.

Direct Access. The ability of a disk drive positioner to move the read/write head directly to the track which the computer wishes to access.

Disk Drive Unit. The peripheral device that spins the disk and reads information from and writes information to the disk storage medium.

DOS (Disk Operating System). The set of instructions needed by the computer to operate the disk drive.

Double Density. The ability to pack information on a floppy disk at twice the normal capacity.

Floppy Disk. A thin, mylar, record-shaped disk housed in a protective cardboard jacket. The magnetic surface can store large amounts of information for microcomputer use.

Go Down. A slang term meaning to stop functioning.

Hard Disk. A metallic, record-shaped disk usually hermetically sealed from the environment. The magnetic surface can store large amounts of information for microcomputer use.

Interface Controller and Formater. The electronic device that interprets signals from the CPU and which controls the position of the read/ write head, formats the data on the disk, and implements handshake routines (programs).

Internal Memory. The electrical circuits within the computer that allow the microcomputer to retain information. Internal memory consists of ROM and RAM.

K. Abbreviation for kilobyte.

Kilobyte. 1,024 bytes (characters) of information.

Load. To transfer information into the computer.

Main Memory. RAM and ROM. See *Internal Memory.*

Medium. A secondary storage magnetic surface, e.g. tape, floppy disk, and hard disk.

Memory. The circuits or devices that can store information for the computer to use.

Peripheral. An input or output device attached to a microcomputer, e.g, keyboard, disk drive, monitor.

Positioner. The arm in the floppy disk drive that moves the read/write head to the proper track on the disk.

RAM (Random-Access Memory). Computer memory. The contents of RAM can be stored and transferred very rapidly to and from the CPU. The scratch pad for the CPU where information is stored temporarily. RAM is alterable and is erased when the computer is turned off.

Read/Write Head. The component of the floppy disk drive that rests on the disk to transfer information. Its function is similar to that of a needle on a record player.

Removable Cartridge. A type of hard disk that allows the disk to be removed and replaced by other hard disks.

ROM (Read-Only Memory). Memory that is preprogrammed with the basic repetitive instructions necessary to operate the computer. ROM is permanent and not erasable.

Secondary Storage. The tape, floppy disk, and hard disk memory systems used by a microcomputer to store large amounts of information.

Track. Defined area on a disk where information is stored. Tracks are arranged in concentric circles on the disk.

9

SELECTING A PRINTER

The microcomputer printer is the weakest link in the input-processing-output chain. Because the printer is expensive and the peripheral device most likely to break, the features must be carefully weighed. The buyer should determine what special features are required and what level of quality will suffice.

Printers can be evaluated on ten factors:

Print quality
Paper feed
Paper size/type
Interfaces
Noise
Speed
Size/Weight/Installation

Special Printing Ability
Durability/Service
Price

Print quality is directly related to price. The better the quality of print, the higher the price. There are four common printing methods:

Thermal
Electrostatic
Dot Matrix
Impact (Thimble/Ball/Daisy Wheel)

Thermal printing requires the use of special heat-sensitive paper which is usually more expensive and often difficult to find. Electrostatic printing poses similar problems. Thermal paper is bought in rolls without perforations (see *Pin Feed* and *Tractor Feed*).

Dot matrix printers are most commonly used with home and business microcomputers. The printed characters consist of small dots similar to newspaper print. The quality of the printed character is proportional to the size and number of dots used to create that character. Five, seven, and nine lines of dots per line of print are standard with seven lines being considered acceptable for most report writing applications.

Impact printers (thimble, ball, or daisy wheel) are more expensive and produce a final product of typewriter quality. The ball, thimble, or wheel can be changed to provide different type style. With this flexibility, special printing for foreign languages and engineering symbols is possible.

Printers with only upper-case characters are acceptable for most applications. However, for word processing and correspondence writing, lower-case characters are needed.

True descenders make the printing more readable. A printer has true descenders if the tails on the *y, j, g,* etc. descend below the word. For dot matrix printers, two-dot descenders are more readable than one-dot descenders. True descenders are needed on a letter-quality (typewriter-quality) printer.

Proportional spacing makes letter-quality printing more attractive. With this option the letter *w* will take more space than the letter *i.* Proportional spacing adjusts the space allotted for the letters according to the letter width. Typewriter spacing is usually equal for each letter.

The desired print quality for a printer depends on the user's application and on the amount of money the buyer plans to spend.

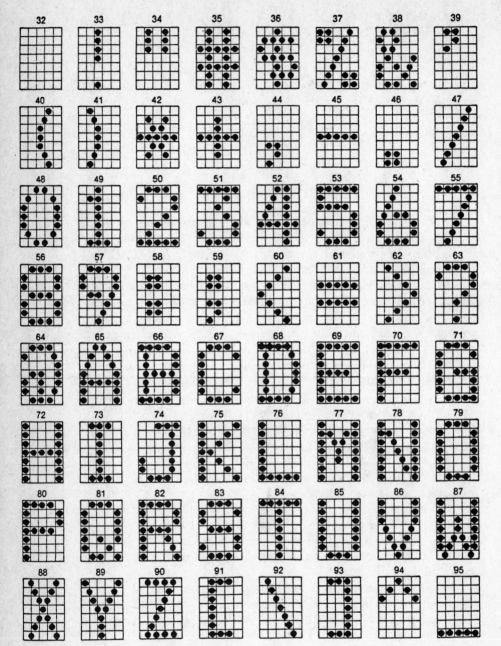

FIGURE 9–1. Dot matrix print style.

ABCDEFGHIJKLMNOPQRSTUVWXYZ

abcdefghijklmnopqrstuvwxyz

123456789!@#$%¢&*()_+:;"?/

FIGURE 9–2. Letter quality print style with true descenders and proportional spacing.

Paper feed is the method for moving the paper through the printer. There are three types of feed:

Friction feed
Pin feed
Tractor feed

Friction feed is similar to a typewriter. The paper is fed by a plastic, steel, or rubber roller (platen). The paper can slip in a friction feed printer. The plastic roller is the least desirable, steel next, and rubber is the best.

Pin feed is built into the printer and not adjustable to different paper width. The roll of paper has a series of holes spaced vertically on both margins. The pins on the roller fit into the holes and guide the paper through the printer like film through a camera. The pin feed keeps the paper aligned and stops slippage.

The *tractor feed* is similar to the pin feed except that it is often removable and can adjust to different paper widths. The tractor feed is desirable for applications where paper alignment and size versatility is required. Tractor feed also provides better registration for graphics where a printer may be required to strike over the same point several times. If the paper is well aligned, multiple striking can be done without causing double images.

Paper size and type must accommodate the user's needs. Thermal printers and electrostatic printers require special paper that is more expensive and often difficult to locate. The tractor and pin feed require special paper with vertically spaced holes on the right and left margins. This paper is more commonly available and thus is usually cheaper than thermal paper.

The number of characters needed to print across an 8½ inch piece of paper is 72–80. If this size of paper is used, the printer must be able to accommodate it. Financial reports may require a column width of 132 characters, which is standard for large computer systems. The report writing operations for many programs require specific column widths and a printer should be purchased based on the needs of the reporting system.

Interfaces are electrical circuits that allow the printer and computer to communicate. If the computer and the printer cannot talk to each other, then the printer is worthless. Some computers require the use of specific printers which the manufacturer designates. This is often because the manufacturer has developed special interfaces for their own printers. Be careful that the printer has the proper interface for the computer it will run on. See the printer operate before buying. Synchronizing the interface is often time-consuming and costly.

Some computers are more versatile and thus can accept printers that plug into both *parallel* and *serial* interfaces. An *RS 232 interface bus* (plug) is an industry standard used on most computers for serial connections. The dealer selling the printer should provide the plugs, cables, and other accessories. Price these items before buying. Accessories can change the entire cost range. Some interfaces are tricky. A mail order printer that costs $400 less but never works is no bargain!

Noise level is an important consideration in the office and home. Have the dealer demonstrate the printer. Seventy decibels is considered maximum for an office application.

Speed, like print quality, is also directly related to price. Faster printers usually cost more and generally make more mistakes. Maintenance may be more expensive for a fast printer. Print speed below 30 *characters per second* (cps) is considered slow, 30–100 cps is medium, and over 100 cps is fast.

There are other capabilities that can make a printer more efficient. *Bidirectional printing* allows the printer to print in both directions: right to left and left to right. This omits the wasted time needed for a carriage to return as on a typewriter. Other printers have the ability to detect blank spaces at the end of a line and proceed to the next line immediately. Some printers continue to travel to the right margin first, which takes more time.

There's nothing like a demonstration to straighten out the cps and lpm (lines per minute). Speed may not be critical if a small amount of printing is required. Select the printer that is fast enough to do the job efficiently and in the price range budgeted.

Size, weight, and installation may be important considerations in the purchase of a printer. If the application requires a portable printer, a 60-pound printer might be too bulky.

Paper feeds into a printer from the back or from the bottom. If the paper feeds in from the bottom, a special table will be needed with a slot under the printer to allow the paper to feed from underneath.

Special printing abilities are required to print foreign languages, engineering documents, and graphics. The printer should be selected on its ability to perform these special functions. If graphics are required, the *dots per inch* (dpi) are critical to the quality of the finished product. See it work before buying!

Durability and service are important if the user depends heavily on large amounts of computer output. Printers are more likely to fail than any other part of the computer. Consider buying a service contract.

Before buying a printer determine:

Who will service it?
Are parts available?
How often might it break?
What is the minimum service charge?
Will the user have to deliver it to the maintenance shop?
Is a loaner available?
What is the expected life (in characters) of the print head?
How expensive is the print head to replace?

The dealer also should provide an interface device. A reputable servicing dealer is a valuable asset.

The price of a computer printer depends on the application. If the application requires speed, durability, letter quality, and versatility, the printer will cost more.

GLOSSARY

Ball. A letter-quality printer head that can be changed to achieve different styles of print.

Bidirectional. The ability of a printer to print in both directions, right to left and left to right.

cps (characters per second). The number of letters, numbers, and symbols a printer can produce in one second.

Daisy Wheel. A letter-quality printer that has the ability to change print style, is durable, and generally more expensive.

Decibel. A measure of loudness. Seventy decibels is considered maximum for office use.

Dot Matrix. A printer that prints the characters as a series of dots similar to newspaper printing.

dpi (dots per inch). The density of the dots created by a dot matrix printer. The greater the dpi, the more clear the image.

Electrostatic Printing. A printing process that forms characters with electric current on special paper.

Friction Feed. A process of moving paper (scrolling) through a printer using only the friction between the printer body and a roller. Typewriters are friction feed devices.

Hard Copy. Printed material produced by a printer.

Interface. An electrical circuit device that connects the computer to the printer (or to other peripheral devices).

lpm (lines per minute). The number of lines a printer can print in one minute.

Parallel. A wiring connection that allows the transmission of information along several pathways at the same time. A standard connection in the microcomputer industry.

Pin Feed. A method for scrolling paper through the printer by using pins on a roller that fit into special holes on the right and left margins of the paper. The pins feed the paper through like film through a camera. The pin feed printer accepts only one width of paper and prevents slippage.

Platen. The plastic, steel, or rubber roller in a friction feed printer; similar to a roller in a typewriter.

RS 232. A wiring connection that allows the transmission of information along a single pathway (serial). A standard connection common to the computer industry.

Serial. A wiring connection that allows the transmission of information along one wire to an output device such as a printer.

Thermal Printing. A printing process that uses heat to activate heat-sensitive paper thus creating a character.

Thimble Printing. See *Ball* and *Daisy Wheel.*

Tractor Feed. A method for moving paper through a printer similar to *Pin Feed* except that the tractor is adjustable to different paper widths and often removable.

True Descenders. A printing style where the tails of letters such as *y, j, g,* descend below the base line. This better simulates letter-quality typewriters.

10

THE TERMINAL DECISION

To make an intelligent decision about a *dumb terminal* requires a little knowledge.

Selecting a terminal means making decisions on what type of *monitor* (visual screen) is needed, whether the terminal must possess special capabilities beyond entering numbers and letters, and what type of *keyboard* is best suited for the job.

THE RIGHT MONITOR

Some of the questions which should be asked when selecting a monitor are:

What is the difference between a TV and CRT?

How many characters per line are displayed?
Does the monitor have color capabilities?
Is a speaker available for audio output?
Is the screen tinted green for eye comfort?
What size is the picture?
Are the controls accessible?

The black and white TV provides an inexpensive method for displaying visual information. The primary drawback to a TV receiver is that the letters, numbers, and special characters are not as clear as on a *cathode ray tube* (CRT). It's difficult for the eye to distinguish a *B* from an *8* or an *N* from an *M* on a TV screen. If the computer application doesn't require frequent reading from the monitor, this may not be a problem. Word processing and graphics applications, however, require the clearer picture resolution provided by the more expensive CRT.

Even with high quality TV receivers, the clarity is limited by the design of the equipment. TVs have wave traps that screen out information that the computer communicates to a CRT. With less information, the TV cannot produce as good an image as a CRT.

Characters per line display capabilities are important for text formating, for displaying financial reports and proposals, and for other applications requiring typewriter line-width capability. The CRT displays up to 80 characters per line and 24 lines per screen, while the TV usually displays only 32 characters per line.

Color is helpful for viewing graphics and artistic computer applications. The ability to draw graphs with different colored lines or to "paint" pictures with color enhances the computer's utility. Some game software requires color capabilities. Ask for a demonstration to evaluate the quality and clarity of the color monitor.

Audio Output allows the computer to give the user sound messages. Word processors often notify the typist when the end of line has been reached by sounding a beep. Computer games provide explosions, tunes for rewards, and discouraging bleeps. Many games would not be fun at all without the audio portion.

Green Tint saves eye strain if many hours are spent at the tube. It's possible to purchase a separate plastic sheet to put in front of the screen. The attachable tinted sheet is less expensive than a special tube that produces a green image. The rigid plastic sheets give less picture distortion than the flexible ones and they are removable.

Sizes of screens range from 9 to 15 inches measured diagonally. Thirteen inches is the most popular and is ideal for most purposes. Larger screens do not project as clear an image as smaller screens.

Controls within easy reach to adjust brightness, focus, and color are a nice convenience. Some terminal controls are inaccessible and cumbersome to use.

"SMART" OR "DUMB"?

Terminals vary in *intelligence* or capability. The application determines the type of terminal needed. Some computers will only run with specified terminals and the dealer should be able to advise of these limitations.

Low end (dumb) *terminals* consist of a monitor, typewriter-type keys, a moderate *baud* (communication) rate (19,200 baud), *cursor addressing and sensing,* a numeric key pad, and lower-case letter capability.

Cursor addressing and sensing is the ability of the computer to locate the position of the cursor and detect its movement. The *cursor* is a bright spot or square that moves on the screen with the entered text and appears where the next entry will be displayed. Cursor addressing allows the computer to detect where data is being entered on the screen. Entering $2.98 on a form projected on the screen in columns 40–43 on row 11 tells the computer where to record the data, for example, sales tax.

Smarter terminals have additional capabilities. The lower-case letters displayed on the monitor have *true descenders.* letters such as *j, g,* and *y* are displayed with their tails descending below the base line. Terminals displaying letters with true descenders are easier to read.

Special function keys are available on smarter terminals. These keys allow the user to utilize more of the computer's capabilities. A word processor program might recognize ESC# as go to new line, ESCT as go to top of page, and CONTROL R as move the cursor to the right margin. These codes allow the manipulation of CRT and printer to achieve the desired text format. The programs purchased determine if these keys are useful or just an added expense.

Video modes of smarter terminals are adjustable. *Reverse video* with black letters on a gray background, dual or triple intensity, blinking, blanking, and underlining are available on smarter terminals.

At even higher "intelligence" levels, the terminal can edit text and store two to eight pages of text. It may also have a variety of transmission (baud) rates. If the terminal has its own *chips* (electronic memory components) like the computer, it can produce and manipulate graphic displays.

Like an expensive typewriter keyboard, the keys should be comfortably spaced and the touch should be positive but not tiring.

If numerical data is entered frequently, a ten-key numerical pad speeds up and improves the accuracy of operation.

Business applications including word processing require the capability of producing upper- and lower-case letters.

Special graphic symbols are very entertaining for the home computer. However, for a business terminal, having graphic symbols may require giving up capabilities needed in the office.

The fast typist needs *rollover* capability so the keyboard will register the next key typed even though the first key may not have returned to its resting state. The fast typist will override a keyboard without rollover and thus will have to slow down or lose data.

Touch switches are available for applications where dirt or contamination are problems. The keyboard is covered with a sheet of flexible plastic like some of the electronic word games. This sealed environment preserves the integrity of the electronics but is not practical for volumes of input. The typist needs kinesthetic feedback from the fingers to know where the fingers are positioned and if a key has been properly struck.

TERMINAL OR MODULAR?

Keyboards can be purchased separately from the CRT or TV. If they are packaged together in a single unit, they are called a *terminal*. It doesn't make any difference in what form they are purchased—individually or as a unit. However, the terminal may be more convenient to use.

MATCH THE APPLICATION

The terminal must match the application for the computer. TV vs. CRT, smart vs. dumb, components vs. terminals are all weighed against the needs of the user and the requirements of the programs.

Baud. The rate at which the keyboard can send information to the computer (measured in *bits* per second).

Bit. The smallest unit of memory in a microcomputer. Physically an on-or-off, yes-or-no state within the computer.

Byte. A unit of measure of information equivalent to one character, letter, or number.

CRT (Cathode Ray Tube). A TV-type tube for displaying video information. The CRT has the capability of producing a much clearer picture than a regular TV.

Chip. An electrical component of the computer.

Cursor. A bright dot or square that appears on the video screen and indicates where the next piece of information will be recorded or where the next action will take place (follow the bouncing ball).

Cursor Addressing and Sensing. The ability of the computer to locate the position of the cursor and detect its movement.

Dumb. A terminal that has only basic functions and limited memory.

Intelligence. The amount of ability built into the terminal. Low end (dumb) terminals have little ability beyond sending electrical signals to the computer. "Smart" terminals may be able to do editing and store up to eight pages of information.

Keyboard. A typewriter-type configuration used to enter information into the computer. It may also include a ten-key pad and special function keys.

Monitor. A TV screen or CRT used to display video information.

Reverse Video. The ability of a CRT or TV to display dark characters on a gray background instead of white characters on a black background.

Rollover. The ability of a keyboard to register a second keyed entry before the first key has returned to its resting position. This prevents a fast typist from overriding the terminal and losing information.

Smart. A terminal that has chips which give it some capabilities similar to a small computer.

Special Function Keys. Keys on the keyboard which allow the user to utilize more of the computer's capabilities to format text. These keys serve as codes to instruct the computer to do standard functions, e.g. ESCT might tell the monitor or printer to skip to the top of the next page.

Terminal. The combination in one unit of a keyboard and a monitor.

Touch Switches. Special switches used for keyboards that are sealed against a dirty environment. A flexible plastic sheet covers the switches similar to a child's electronic spelling game.

True Descenders. The ability that allows a monitor to display the tails on letters like *y, g,* and *j* below the base line.

11

HARDWARE FROM ACCUMULATOR TO VLSI

BELMONT COLLEGE LIBRARY

Some microcomputer users want to know more about the *hardware* (equipment) than the typical user. For those who have a need or craving for technical information, this chapter is a glossary of hardware terms not found elsewhere in this book.

GLOSSARY OF HARDWARE TERMS

Accumulator. Another term for register. A dedicated storage location within the CPU. Most microcomputers have one accumulator. The number of accumulators is directly related to the processing speed.

Address. A way of referencing a memory location, that is, identifying it. (*Addressing* is the process of accessing a specific memory location.)

Analogue. A type of computer which does not work by detecting an on-or-off state (1 or 0 in binary code) but works with states that change more smoothly, for example voltage changes. Often used in equipment control and scientific applications.

ALU (Arithmetic Logic Unit). The part of the processor which performs arithmetical and logic operations.

ANSI (American National Standards Institute). An organization which defines the specifications of high level programming languages, ASCII code, etc.

ASCII (American Standard Code for Information Interchange). A coded representation for alphanumeric characters in binary (base 2) counting system. For example, the letter *A* might have a numerical value of 65 and be represented by the binary number of 1000001. The binary code is understood by the processor.

Arithmetic Functions—ALU (Arithmetic-Logic Unit). That part of the processor which performs arithmetic and logic functions. For example, add, subtract, multiply, and divide are arithmetic and *and, or, not* are logic operations.

Baud. The rate at which information passes through a communication line represented in bits per second: 1200 *baud* is equal to 1200 bits per second. This commonly applies to the rate at which peripherals such as terminals and printers can send and receive information.

BCD (Binary Coded Decimal). A method for representing alphanumerics using bit structures (see *ASCII*).

Binary Logic. A method for representing numbers to the base 2. This method of counting uses only symbols 1 and 0. A specified pattern of 1s and 0s can represent numbers which stand for ASCII codes for characters. The processor responds with an electrical on or off state when it receives 1s and 0s.

Buffer. A block of memory where the CPU temporarily puts information so that a second piece of equipment that works at a different speed can find it when needed.

Bus. Wires or electrical components that allow electrical signals (information) to travel to different parts of the computer system; a set of connections.

Digital. Opposite of analogue; a system or device using discrete signals to represent numerical data, usually binary code. Almost all computer operations are digital.

Dump. Transfer of information from main memory into secondary storage or to another output peripheral.

Duplex. Transmitting information in two directions at once.

Enable. To switch a device on; setting the processor to accept signals.

Handshake. Signals or pulses that establish synchronization between an asynchrous Input/Output unit (I/O) and the computer.

HITS (Hobbyist's Interchange Tape Standard). Data recording standard for cassette tapes.

IC (Integrated Circuit). A tiny electronic circuit contained in a single silicon chip. A technology that makes microcomputers possible.

Joystick. A lever that can be tilted any direction (360 degrees) and which controls the position of the cursor on the CRT. Used in graphics and computer games.

LCD (Liquid Crystal Display). Technology used for displaying the time on a watch; will be used for screens eventually.

LED (Light Emitting Diode). An electronic component which provides a digital read-out similar to the time display on a watch (often red).

Light Pen. A photoelectric device which can detect the presence of light at a particular point on the CRT. It looks like a pen and has a cable which connects it to a controller. When placed on the screen, the controller detects where the pen is located. Depending on the program, the computer will take appropriate action, for example, the selection of a response or the drawing of a character.

Logic. Systemized interconnection of discrete components in the processor; logic functions include *and, or,* and *not.*

LSI (Large-Scale Integration). Electrical circuitry with a large number of logical operations per component.

Microsecond. One millionth of a second (M).

Millisecond. One thousandth of a second.

MODEM (MOdulator/DEModulator). A device which converts data from the processor to a signal that can be transmitted over communication (telephone) lines and reconverts the data at the receiving end so that the processor can use the information.

MOS (Metal Oxide Semiconductor). Widespread technology used in microcomputers which made LSI possible.

Mother Board. An electronic assembly board on which printed circuits (PC) can be interconnected through a *bus.*

MPU (MicroProcessor Unit). The electronic circuits in the microcomputers which perform arithmetic and logic functions and control I/O devices.

Nanosecond (ns). One billionth of a second.

Nibble. One half of a *byte*; 4 *bits* on an 8 *bit* computer.

Noise. Unwanted electrical signals; interference.

Off-Line. Disconnected from the computer or not communicating with the computer; for example a keypunch machine is an off-line piece of equipment; if a printer is turned off, it's off-line.

On-Line. Connected to and communicating with the computer; for example a printer in operation.

Optical Wand. A bar code reader which usually feeds signals into a cassette tape recorder. Used by grocers to read the pricing and inventory information on packages and containers.

Overwrite. To store information in a location already containing data in such a manner that destroys the original information.

Parallel Interface. The flow of information where all *bits* in a "word" arrive and pass through the interface at once; a word of 8 bits needs 8 wires in and 8 wires out of the parallel plug or socket; faster than *serial interface*; generally used with printers; cannot travel as far as *serial.*

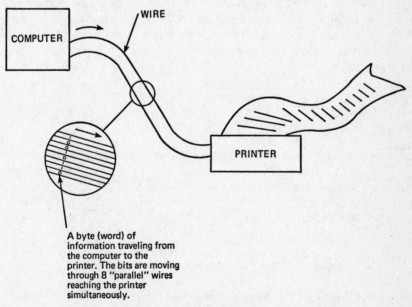

A byte (word) of information traveling from the computer to the printer. The bits are moving through 8 "parallel" wires reaching the printer simultaneously.

FIGURE 11-1. Transfer of information through a parallel interface.

PC (Printed Circuit). An electronic circuit constructed on an insulated board. The electronic parts such as transistors and resistors are attached to the board which has metal strips etched (printed) onto it to connect each component. This rigid, wireless construction is compact and easily mass-produced.

Plotter. A mechanical device which receives signals from the processor to draw graphs, pictures, etc.

Pointer. A register or accumulator which holds the address of the next memory location to be accessed by the program. Pointers work like a book mark so the computer can "find its place."

Ports. An electrical outlet in the computer; for example, a plug receptor for a terminal (I/O device).

Protocol. Set of conventions for the exchange of information between I/O devices.

RS 232. A serial *bus* (see *Serial Interface*); standard for the industry.

Register. See *Accumulator.*

S 100. 100 pin *bus*; popular connection; standards for all pin functions not uniformly defined.

Serial Interface. An electrical configuration where information travels "single file" through the connections; the binary code travels in sequence or single channel; widely used with printer and terminal connections to the computer; slower than *parallel interface*; simpler and can travel longer distances.

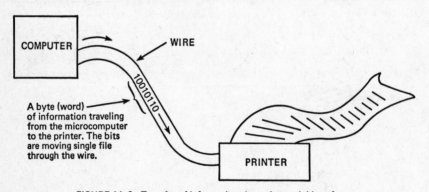

FIGURE 11-2. Transfer of information through a serial interface.

Stack. Temporary memory in main memory which automatically keeps track of locations using a stack pointer.

Status. The state of a particular I/O device representing its condition, for example, ready to receive information or ready to send information.

Throughput Rate. The operating speed with which a computer processes data and produces a result.

Time Sharing. Simultaneous use of CPU by two or more users. The processor handles the demands sequentially, but it is so fast that it appears to be simultaneous.

VLSI (Very Large Scale Integration). An electronics technology which allows the compacting of large numbers of components into microchips.

IV

HOW TO SELECT
MICROCOMPUTER
SOFTWARE

12

SOFTWARE
ISN'T SO HARD

Software is the instructions that tell the computer what to do and how to do it. Good software can make a computer of moderate quality work well. Poor software can make a sophisticated computer inoperative.

Software selection is the most important decision the computer buyer makes. It is the equivalent of hiring an employee. Skills and knowledge are the important considerations in an employment decision. Likewise, the ability, knowledge, and efficiency of the software outweigh the physical characteristics of microcomputers.

HOW HARDWARE AND SOFTWARE INTERACT

The best way to remember the meaning of *software* is to remember the nature of the word "soft." The equipment (hardware) is made of "hard" metal and plastic and the programmed instructions (software) are stored on paper, tape, or floppy disk which are soft and flexible.

Complicated? Not really. Think of the human brain as the computer or *hardware*. Reading a how-to book tells the brain (CPU) procedures for doing something, e.g., baking a cake. The eyes (*disk read/ write head*) receive the light from the cookbook page (*floppy disk*) and send the data to the brain's short-term memory storage area (RAM). There the brain (CPU) can quickly call on the information as it bakes the cake (executes the instructions).

If the brain (CPU) wants to double the recipe and keep a record of the new quantities, it stores the calculated results in short-term memory (RAM). Then it commands the hand (*disk read/write head*) to record the new amounts in the cookbook (*floppy disk*). If the double recipe is used again, the data is available in the cookbook (*secondary storage*) at a later date without recalculation.

The physical work is performed by the parts of the body (*hardware*) such as eyes, hands, and brain. The instructions (*software*) are stored temporarily in short term memory (RAM) and then written on a page in the cookbook (*floppy disk*). The instructions must be put (*loaded*) into the brain (*hardware*) before the body can do any useful work. If it wants, the brain can alter the information, in this case the quantities in the recipe, and store the new data in the cookbook (*secondary storage*) for future reference.

The human brain has instructions in it that work automatically. These instructions control our breathing, blood pressure, and other bodily functions. Some of these basic functions make us conscious of the outside world, "awake," so to speak. The computer also has built-in instructions (*firmware*) which are called ROM. *Read-Only Memory* isn't altered with use nor can it be erased. ROM prepares the CPU to "wake up" and be ready to receive information and further instructions.

The software is the collective instructions that tell the computer what to do. The instructions are listed sequentially in what is called a *program*. A portion of a program is called a *routine*. The programs are usually stored in *secondary storage* such as *cassette tape, floppy disk*, or *hard disk*. When the user is ready for a particular set of instructions, the information is *loaded* into the computer's memory (RAM) where the CPU can utilize the data.

TYPES OF SOFTWARE

There are two types of software used by the microcomputer. *Applications software* tells the computer how to perform a specific function, e.g., inventory control and payroll. *Systems software* is the collective information that tells the computer how to communicate, how to relate to the peripherals (printer, terminal, etc.), and how to operate internally.

In our cooking analogy, the applications software would be the instructions from the cookbook. The systems software would be the instructions the brain has for reading the cookbook, for understanding the language it's written in, for controlling the parts of the body necessary to perform the functions of baking the cake (arms, legs, hands, etc.), and for writing the new quantities on the page for future reference.

SELECTING SOFTWARE: A JOB INTERVIEW

Selecting software for a microcomputer is similar to conducting a job interview. The employer wants to evaluate the capabilities of a prospective employee to do the job.

The software buyer wants manuals, applications programs, and operating systems which will do a particular job. The software must be compatible with the equipment and cost effective.

WHAT JOB MUST THE APPLICATION SOFTWARE PERFORM?

A job description should be written for the microcomputer. Just like looking for an employee, it's difficult to find a computer that can do everything. So avoid looking for the "icing on the cake." Get applications and systems software that will do the bulk of the work.

IS THERE ENOUGH MEMORY TO DO THE JOB?

The *internal memory* (RAM and ROM) determines how large an application system can be accommodated by the computer. In a typical business system, the distribution of memory in a 64K (kilobytes) microcomputer is as follows:

Monitor function—2K

Operating system—30K
Language—10–15K
RAM (Short-term memory)—20K

A kilobyte represents 1,026 characters: 64K is 65,536 characters. The above example shows that as the operating system occupies more room, there is less room available for RAM. If the program has a large number of instructions, more RAM is utilized, leaving less room for data storage. If the language is too complicated and requires a lot of internal memory, there is less RAM available for the application to occupy.

The software buyer must balance the capacity of the computer against the operating system, programming language efficiency, software, and volume of data.

IS THE SYSTEM COMPATIBLE WITH THE COMPUTER?

Not all software runs on all computers. The microcomputer dealer or the sales literature from the software manufacturer should help clarify which software is compatible with the computer.

If the computer is purchased for specific needs, such as payroll, accounts receivable/payable, etc., then it is advisable to find the best software packages before buying the computer.

CHECK OUT SPECIAL PROBLEMS

If the application requires extensive processing (sorting, calculations, searches for information, etc.), make sure the software is efficient for large volumes of data. If the user needs to search files for information, e.g. looking up inventory levels, the software should do the job in a reasonable amount of time. Ask for a demonstration with large amounts of data. Searching through and sorting small files is easy for almost any computer. The acid test is a volume test.

SHOULD YOU PROGRAM IT YOURSELF?

Every "canned" program can be improved on for a given application. By nature, prewritten programs must appeal to a large variety of users and may appear on the surface to be too general for use by one particular company. Besides, programming your own applications sounds like fun. But fun things can lead to trouble.

Before training a new employee with no experience, it's wise to first see what is available on the market. After all, this new "employee" will have a great deal of responsibility and therefore should be reliable and trustworthy. Besides, how much time is available to do on-the-job training in the most minute detail?

Designing a customized system for a computer is similar to training an inexperienced employee. To avoid costly, extra work, find out first if a commercial package is available that will do the job. Check with the dealer who sold (or is going to sell) the computer. Get references from the dealer of customers who are using the system in a similar application and CHECK THEM OUT.

If a commercial system is not available, decide if there is time and money to do it yourself. Do you need the application immediately? It may take many months to work out all of the details. In the meantime, who will do the regular work and who will do the programming? Do you want to pay the price for being the first user?

Will the custom programming be as sophisticated and error-free as packaged systems? For example, quality commercial systems have built-in checks and balances that detect errors in input. If a letter is entered where a number belongs, the computer will notify the operator of the mistake. Will the custom-written program run as efficiently and be as versatile?

Will the programmer prepare documentation (manuals) that the user can understand? Good documentation is a training aid and trouble-shooting guide for the operator. Also, if the programs ever need modification, program documentation is essential.

Make certain the application is really that unique. If a standard program with minimal modification can be used to do the bulk of the work, lean in that direction.

DOES THE SOFTWARE HAVE ERROR TRAPS?

Most errors are committed by the operator, not by the computer. If the computer can catch the errors as they are entered, much time and trouble will be saved.

The program should test for the content of certain *fields*. That is, if a numeral is entered in an alphabetical field, the computer indicates that the entry is wrong. Or, the computer checks to see if the FICA amount is reasonable within established numerical limits. *Editing (error detection)* of user mistakes is a key ingredient in the computer software. Custom programming often bypasses this important phase.

FASTEST IS NOT ALWAYS BEST

Most computer time is used entering the information. Therefore, the data entry sequences should be simple and efficient.

Menus are choices presented to the user before proceeding. For example the computer might present the following menu:

Select Brand
1. FORD
2. CHEVROLET
3. CADILLAC
4. CHRYSLER
5. DATSUN

After the user has entered 2 for CHEVROLET, the monitor then displays the following menu:

Select Year
1. BEFORE 1980
2. 1980
3. 1981
4. 1982
5. 1983
6. 1984
7. 1985

And on and on the computer can elicit responses. The inexperienced user will find this helpful. But the frequent user may find prompting boring and time-consuming.

Another method for entering data is filling in the blanks as follows:

Enter the following data
Make__ __ __ __ __ __ __ __ __ __ __ __ __
Year__ __ __ __
Style__ __ __ __
Color__ __
Condition__ __

Prompting, in the first example, produces fewer operator errors. Filling in the blanks requires more disk accesses and operator time. If the floppy disk is accessed repeatedly while the program is running, more time will be needed to perform the job. Disk access takes up to 2 seconds per incident, whereas the internal memory operates in millionths of a second. The user must determine which process is best suited to the needs.

SEE A DEMONSTRATION

The real proof lies in a demonstration. See the computer operating with the application. Enter some data to test the efficiency and error checks. Inspect the reports or output to determine if they give the information needed for the application. Compare the job description to the performance of the software. If the bulk of the job is done well and in a timely manner, the software will work.

GLOSSARY

Applications Software. Instructions that tell the computer how to perform a specific function, e.g. inventory control and payroll.

CPU. The central "brain" of the computer that controls the peripherals and does the analytical and arithmetical calculations.

Cassette Tape. A secondary storage medium for data and programs. The cassette is similar to the tape used with a cassette recorder for recording music.

Disk Access. The process of retrieving or writing information to the disk by the disk drive. The access time for the floppy disk is from 1/10 second to 2 seconds compared to millionths of a second for internal memory.

Editing (Error Detection). Protection built in a good program that tests the data entered by the operator. The computer checks to see if the amounts are reasonable, e.g., FICA amount on a pay check.

Floppy Disk. A secondary storage medium for data and programs. The disk is shaped like a 45 rpm record, is flexible, and is made of material similar to recording tape.

Hardware. The equipment or electrical components of a microcomputer system.

Internal Memory. The electrical circuits within the computer that allow the microcomputer to retain information. The CPU can access internal memory in millionths of a second. The internal memory consists of ROM (*Read-Only Memory*) and RAM (*Random-Access Memory*).

K (Kilobyte). A unit of measure for information which is roughly equal to 1,026 characters. A *byte* is equal to one character.

Load. Transferring information to the computer from secondary storage such as floppy disk or to the disk from the computer, e.g., *load* a program.

Menu. A list of choices presented by the software which represents a decision point in the running of the program. The selection of a particular item displayed on the CRT allows the computer to proceed in the desired direction. Menus tend to reduce operator errors by simplifying operator response.

Program. The step-by-step instructions that tell the computer what to do.

RAM (Random-Access Memory). The short-term internal memory components of the computer.

ROM (Read-Only Memory). The permanent memory component of the computer.

Routine. A portion of a program that performs a subfunction.

Secondary Storage. Information storage devices external to the computer, e.g., floppy disk and cassette tape. Large amounts of information can be retained in secondary storage without consuming the computer's limited internal memory.

Software. The instructions that tell the computer what to do and how to do it.

Systems Software. The collective information that tells the computer how to communicate, how to relate to the peripherals (printer, terminal, etc.), and how to operate internally.

13

HOW TO EVALUATE
DOCUMENTATION
MANUALS

Documentation is something which a programmer does not do well, a hobbiest never does, and a novice cannot understand.

The manuals for operating equipment and *executing* (running) programs are critical for training, implementation, and systems design. If this *documentation* is poor, extra money or time will be required for improving the manuals or for starting-up processes.

The microcomputer industry has had to respond to the need for user self-instruction. The dealer cannot afford to give free start-up support. Therefore, the user must be able to rely on user manuals and prompted programming to make the system operational.

Before buying, the user should examine software and hardware documentation and evaluate the quality of the package.

WHY DO YOU NEED MANUALS?

Users have several reasons to need manuals: to teach themselves how to use the computer, peripheral devices, and programs; to find specific answers to problems; and for quick reference. The experience level of the user determines the level at which the manual must be written. The beginner has tutorial needs while the experienced operator may want to quickly look up a code. The manuals should be organized so that these different levels of need are met.

WHAT KINDS OF MANUALS DO YOU NEED?

Systems manuals describe how an entire system works, e.g., a financial package including accounts payable, receivable, payroll, etc. It tells the purpose of the system and the relationships between routines (parts of programs). The system flow is laid out and data formats are defined. The systems documentation describes the function, purpose, and logic of the system as well as giving an overview of how the system operates. The systems manual is the umbrella for the operator and user manuals.

User manuals tell what information must be entered, how output reports are formated, and what a particular function will do.

Operator manuals tell how to run the equipment and programs.

TEN WAYS TO EVALUATE DOCUMENTATION

1) What Level of Computer Expertise is Needed to Use the Manual?

The manual should be written for the people using the computer. A quick review of the manual will indicate if it is written for the novice. Examine the first few pages to determine if there is a lot of *jargon* (computer terms and abbreviations). Must the reader know computer basics to understand the manual? Are the basics explained in detail or briefly summarized?

Example Requiring Some Knowledge:

The correct system start-up procedure is to first turn on the computer, then the video terminal, and then the printer. Place the diskette in the disk drive unit and boot the system.

Example Requiring Little Knowledge:

1. Flip the switch on the back of the computer into the up position. This will turn the computer on.
2. Flip the switch on the back of the terminal (keyboard and monitor) to the up position. This will turn the terminal on.
3. Press the printer on/off switch to the down position. The switch is located on the left side panel as you face the front. This turns the printer on.

The above examples illustrate the difference in detail required to communicate effectively to users with varying expertise levels. Examine the manual to determine if it is written appropriately for the people operating the computer.

2) What Language Level Is Used?

Are the words short and common? Are the sentences short and simple? Short words and sentences are easier to read and comprehend. If sentences exceed seventeen words, they are too long. If jargon and multiple-syllable words are frequent, the manual will be difficult to follow.

Example of Difficult Language Level:

Edit is used to make typographical corrections to a line. Typing E60, for example, will display line 60 with the cursor after the last character or space in the line. From this position the cursor can be moved back to any point in the line by typing the *backspace* (or *control-H*) key. The *shifted backspace* (or *control-L* or *control-P*) will move the cursor forward (to the right).

Example of Easily Read Instructions:

Edit is designed to permit changes and corrections to the text you have already typed. To edit a portion of a line, type the letter E, the line number, and hit *return,* e.g. E60 return. The monitor will display the line you wish to change. The *cursor* (white square) will appear at the right margin. To move the cursor to the part of the line you wish to correct, press the *backspace key.* The cursor will continue to move from right to left until you release the key. To move the cursor to the right, press the *shift key.* While holding the *shift key* down, press the *backspace key.* The cursor will stop moving toward the right margin when the keys are released . . .

3) Are The Pages Organized and Easy to Read?

The type should be legible and dark enough to see without strain. Black ink on white paper is easier on the eyes than a wierd color that is hard to read or duplicate. A combination of both upper- and lower-case letters is easier to read than all caps. Subheadings enable the reader to find a topic quickly. Double-spaced type and an uncluttered appearance are a definite plus and a sign of professionalism.

4) Is the Organization Clear and Easy to Follow?

The writer should express the information in an organized, properly sequenced, clear way. The logic should be apparent. The procedural steps should be in proper order. For example, the manual should tell the user to "push the button and type *D*," not "type *D* after pushing the button."

    References are useful for finding information quickly. The manual should have a good *index* and *glossary*. The *table of contents* should have enough detail to be useful. If it's a large manual, it should have reference *tabs*.

5) Does the Documentation Have Summary Lists?

The manual should have a summary of commands and error codes. Sometimes when the computer is told to do something, it will respond with a message like "Error #4." The user should be able to thumb to a page in the manual that will explain what the message means and how to correct the problem or to respond. For example, Error #4 might mean that the door to the disk drive unit has been left open. To correct the problem the operator must shut the door.

6) Are the Illustrations Helpful?

Illustrations should range from the simple to the complex. For example, an illustration of a computer might consist of four boxes with lines connecting them. The next illustration might break down the functions

DRAWING 1:

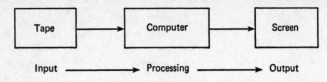

DRAWING 2:

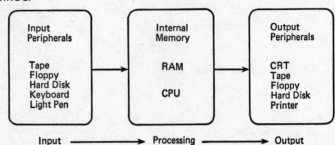

FIGURE 13-1. The right way to illustrate a manual: Move from the simple to the complex.

of one box (e.g., the disk drive) and show how each part relates to the whole.

The same configuration should be used from one diagram to another. If the printer is represented as a rectangle in one diagram, it should not be a circle in the next. If the illustration has the parts numbered to match a keyed list, the numbers should proceed in an orderly fashion around the figures, e.g. clockwise.

Illustrations of sample reports should have actual data, not just dashes or Xs. The numbers are much better since they make it easier for the user to analyze or trouble-shoot a problem.

7) Is the Information Relevant to Your Application?

Does the writer stick to the important information or is superfluous text included? Irrelevant information creates extra reading and makes it difficult for the user to zero in on specific data. The user's manual, for example, should not have information on the way the routine is programmed.

DRAWING 1:

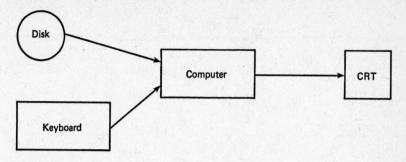

DRAWING 2: INCONSISTENT WITH DRAWING #1—CONFUSING

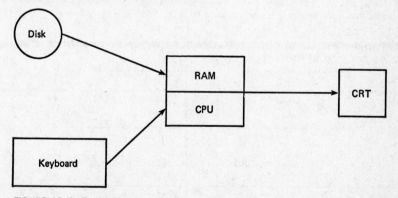

DRAWING 3: CONSISTENT WITH DRAWING #1

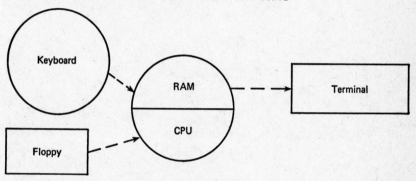

FIGURE 13–2. The right way to illustrate a manual: Be consistent with the use of terminology and symbols from one illustration to the next.

DRAWING 1: CORRECT—COUNTER CLOCKWISE ORDER

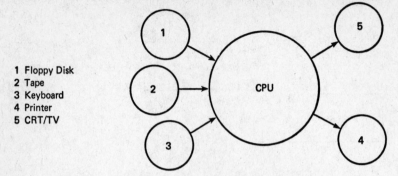

1 Floppy Disk
2 Tape
3 Keyboard
4 Printer
5 CRT/TV

DRAWING 2: INCORRECT—RANDOM ORDER

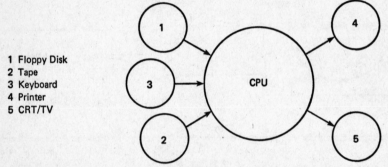

1 Floppy Disk
2 Tape
3 Keyboard
4 Printer
5 CRT/TV

FIGURE 13–3. The right way to illustrate a manual: Keyed numbers should proceed in an orderly fashion around the drawing.

FIGURE 13–4. The right way to illustrate a manual: Reports should have actual numbers entered rather than dashes or Xs.

CORRECT		INCORRECT	
ITEM	COST	ITEM	COST
Parts	$43.62	Parts	$XX.XX
Labor	20.00	Labor	XX.XX
Sls Tx	1.00	Sls Tx	X.XX
Sub Tot	$64.62	Sub Tot	$XX.XX
Delivery	0	Delivery	XX.XX
Other	0	Other	XX.XX
Total	$64.62	Total	$XX.XX

8) Is Routing or Redundancy Held To a Minimum?

Routing or referring to other sections of the manual can create confusion and frustration. However, a balance should exist between routing and redundancy. The reader doesn't want to read the same information over and over either.

Look for references to other sections of the text, e.g., See *Control-T*, page 34. If these instructions appear frequently, particularly within one function, the manual will be difficult to use.

9) Is the Technical Quality Good?

The manual should meet the user's needs. It should serve the purpose it says it does. The information should be organized in a high to low manner, i.e., with the big picture presented first, followed by the details. The answers should be complete and explained in the proper depth. Incomplete answers or too much detail confuse and bore the reader. Definitions and explanations should be clear. The writer should present lists of tools and supplies needed before telling how to use them.

10) Does the Manual Give the Reader Indigestion?

Too much, too fast leaves the novice cold and shivering.

GOOD PROGRAM DOCUMENTATION SAVES YOU MONEY

Programs need good documentation to save operating, *debugging,* and maintenance time. (Debugging is computerese for finding a logic error in a program and correcting it. A *bug* is a logic error within a program.)

If the programs are distributed to a number of locations, documentation is even more essential. The manual should assume that the user knows very little. The descriptions should include labels, procedures, descriptions of the *data base,* and when and who wrote it. (A data base is a collection of data used by a computer system.)

Most people who buy a computer or software evaluate the catalogs, equipment, and the dealer's competence. In actual fact, next to the quality of the programs, the quality of the documentation plays the greatest role in the efficient installation of the system.

GLOSSARY

Bug. A logic error in a program.

Data Base. A collection of data used by a computer system.

Debug. To find and correct a logic error (*bug*) in a program.

Documentation. The manuals for operating equipment and programs. Manuals which are essential to the training and implementation of the computer system.

Execute. To run a program.

Jargon. Technical computer terms or abbreviations, e.g. DOS, boot, field, file.

Operator Manual. The manual that tells the user how to run the equipment or the operating programs.

Program. A set of sequential instructions which tells the computer what to do and when to do it.

Routine. A program within a program.

Systems Manual. The manual that describes how an entire system works. The umbrella for the operator and user manuals.

User Manual. The manual which tells what information must be entered, how output reports are formated, and what a particular program will do.

14

GAMES COMPUTERS PLAY

Ever dreamed of going on a treasure hunt, or of following clues and facing perils from one adventure to another? Ever wanted a chess partner at 3 A.M. during a sleepless night, or wished you could play the new electronic arcade games, flying space ships and shooting lasers hour after hour without spending all of your extra money? Ever wanted to write music but don't have understanding neighbors or room in the apartment for a piano?

With the microcomputer and some good game software, all of these dreams are possible, and more. The important thing is not to waste money on games with little play value.

Buying computer games is, in some ways, like shopping for any game. The game should be designed for a certain age level, for a specified number of players, for challenge, sport, competition, excitement, or learning.

Looking at the packaging on computer games tells the buyer very little. Commercial artists attract the buyer's attention with colorful displays, laughing players, and tidbit information. However, the meaningful qualities such as the strategy, complexity, variety, and play value often must be assessed after the purchase.

Because computer game software is expensive, the buyer should try to find out as much as possible about the game before getting it. Demonstrations, reviews in magazines, and recommendations from satisfied customers are all valuable in making a computer game selection. A good dealer will have the game available to play on a demonstrator computer.

The variety of games on the market is endless: war and space simulation, board games, sports, gambling and card games, shoot-em-up games, arcade style games, puzzle and strategy games, personal enlightenment, entertainment, art and music composition.

Fantasy and adventure games are role-playing games that require quick wits. Examples are Haunted House, the Wizard and the Princess, treasure hunts, slaying monsters, damsels in distress, and doomed cities. The player is the eyes and hands of the knight in shining armor or the treasure hunter. Ghosts, monsters, traps, and dead-ends thwart the player's progress to the goal. The hero or heroine works his or her way through the maze until the monster is defeated, the princess is saved, or the treasure is found.

War and space simulation games such as Galactic Empire, Computer Ambush, and other simulated battles provide excitement for the sharpshooter and strategist. Spaceships, airplanes, and other targets try to elude pursuit. Explosions, surprise attacks, and changing conditions keep the "commander" alert and struggling.

Board games such as monopoly, poker, hearts, backgammon, chess, checkers, and other popular parlour games have kept people entertained for centuries. Playing against the computer provides an odd-hour companion or expert competition for the accomplished player. The computer should do more than just move the pieces unless that itself is a complex process. The software should interact with the player(s) in a positive way.

Gambling and card games such as craps, roulette, crazy eights, bridge, and solitaire also lend themselves well to computer simulation.

Sports such as bowling, tennis, basketball, baseball, boxing, football, and golf give the armchair sports fan an opportunity to defeat the greatest quarterbacks or the top tennis pro. Just think, no bruises, sore muscles, or freezing fingers.

Arcade games and **shoot-em-up games** such as Bomber, Super Invaders, Laser Turrett, Tank War, Trapshoot, Darts and Balloons,

Pinball, and Dual Race are making millions of dollars for arcade businesses. Now these games are available in the home with a microcomputer. The software may be expensive but a game that provides hour after hour of fun is much cheaper than putting quarters in a slot.

Personal enlightenment software allows the user to develop horoscopes in minutes, to predict the future with ancient tarot, to study biorhythms, to compose music, and to develop computer graphics in color. The serious or the casual user can enjoy these games with family or friends.

How can the buyer be sure if a piece of game software will be worth the price? Most games are fun for the first 10 or 15 minutes. However, for lasting play value, the software must stand up to more critical examination. The buyer should ask some questions before investing.

Can I use the game on my equipment?   The information on the packaging of the *tape* or *diskette* should indicate what machines the game will work on. Often the same game is available for a variety of equipment. Graphics and music composition will require special printers, CRTs or sound output creating devices.

Does the game make me want to play it again?   Is it fun? Can I play it over and over without getting bored? Good game software tells the player the previous high score, gives the player a goal to shoot for, provides variety, bonus points, increasing difficulty in succeeding games, fancy displays or music to reward success. These devices make the player want to continue.

Can I understand the rules and instructions?   Does the program prompt the new player through the rules or procedures? Good software will lead the new player step-by-step through the game rules by giving instructions, asking questions, and offering specific choices. The experienced player should be able to avoid the prompting for repeat sessions. The instructions should be clear and complete.

Is it difficult enough but not too difficult?   A game that can never be mastered may be a challenge to one person and a disappointment to another. The level of difficulty should be variable or should automatically increase with continued play. This flexibility allows the user to play at a level that is challenging but not overwhelming. A tested previous high score will be more motivating than some standard set by the game. A player who can never win or cannot see an improvement over previous games will become frustrated.

Is there flexibility for changing the rules to make different games?   If the software can be modified to vary the play, the software is worth more.

Is it rewarding to win?   Are there light displays, explosions, bonuses, and praise for winning? What happens if the player loses? With some games the displays for losing, like the ship blowing up, are so spectacular that it is fun to lose. An action recap at the end of play can be studied to determine how the game might have been played better.

Is the game exciting or challenging?   A game should have unexpected and fast action. If the player can anticipate where the next monster will jump onto the screen or where the next target will appear, the play will be boring after a time. The game should have surprises and changes in pace.

If the game can meet most of these requirements, the player will keep coming back for more. The software will be worth the expense.

Users can find games in computer stores on tapes and diskettes, in books, in magazines, and in computer user club libraries. A computer owner who wants to learn more about how the machine works can even write computer game programs.

In summary, a game worth the money will:

Be difficult to master
Give bonus points/extra shots for good performance
Have something to shoot for (previous high score)
Provide variety
Have increasing difficulty
Be unpredictable (to some extent)
Have fast or variable speed action
Make winning better than losing

GLOSSARY

Cassette. See *Tape.*

Diskette. A flexible record made of magnetic tape material used for storing information (in this case the game program).

Display. The picture on the CRT (Cathode Ray Tube—TV type screen).

Program. A set of instructions that tells the computer what to do.

Prompt. Set of instructions that the program displays for the user that tells the user step-by-step what to do to operate the game (or system).

Software. The program or instructions that tell the computer what to do. It is usually stored on a diskette or cassette tape.

Tape. Recording tape in a cassette that has the program stored on it for the game.

15

**EVALUATING
EDUCATIONAL
SOFTWARE**

Microcomputers are used for instruction at home, in the school, and in business. While the needs of kindergarteners and of adult learners vary, the basics of good *software* (instructions which tell the computer what to do and when to do it) span the age continuum. What can the computer do that the teacher cannot? Can the computer relieve teachers and administrators of paperwork? How can the computer alert educators to problems with students?

Which software package will help Jeff with his multiplication tables? Why won't Kimberly use the computer for spelling drill unless her teacher operates it with her? Why does George repeatedly lock up the screen?

These are only a few of the problems with educational micro-computer use. Good instructional software should meet most of the following criteria if it is to be effective and easy to use.

IS THE SOFTWARE RELEVANT TO
THE OBJECTIVES OF THE COURSE?

While this seems obvious on the surface, evaluating the software to determine if it is relevant, if it is appropriate, and if in fact it contributes to the learning process is not an easy task.

The software must fit into the curriculum. If software is not available, then it should be custom-written for the course.

Not only can the three Rs be addressed, but also eye-hand coordination, making rapid responses, problem solving, modeling, and testing values, to mention only a few functions.

Field testing is the only accurate way to determine the effects of the software on learning. However, this process is both time-consuming and expensive. References from customers who use the programs (software) may help in the buying decision.

DOES THE SOFTWARE FOLLOW
GOOD EDUCATIONAL PRACTICE?

Good teaching practices present materials in small, well-sequenced units. For example, addition may be taught using the numbers 1 through 4 prior to proceeding to 5 through 9. Or a course in report writing might begin with an exercise in constructing short sentences before discussing content organization. Microcomputer software should be organized in this same manner.

Learning is enhanced with immediate feedback. That is, if the student knows right away whether or not the answer is correct, the learning process is more effective. Microcomputers are particularly adept at giving immediate feedback.

There are many ways to present feedback. In a classroom situation, however, care must be taken not to make feedback noisy, negative, or too obvious to students in the room. A loud buzz signaling an incorrect response will prove to be both embarassing and a source for classroom giggles.

Passive feedback simply tells the student whether the answer is right or wrong. *Active feedback* might present pleasant graphics on the screen as a reward for good performance. A smiling face or a clown doing a backward somersault are examples of active feedback. *Interactive feedback* rewards the students with fun games to play. For example, if the students score above 80 percent, they get 4 pin balls to shoot. Above 90 percent they get 10 photon torpedoes to fire at the space invaders.

Negative feedback discourages learning. If the computer makes an insulting remark like, "Try again stupid!", it might be funny the first time. But after that, it's wearing. If the program just moves on to the next problem after each correct answer, feedback may not be positive enough to maintain motivation. If the display is more dramatic for making the mistake, for example an elaborate explosion, the student may deliberately make errors to break the boredom. If the incorrect answer is displayed on the screen, it may have a negative effect, for example, a misspelled word. Also, if playing the odds is allowed, learning may not be encouraged.

ARE GRAPHICS USED TO AID LEARNING?

Graphics should aid instruction, not distract from the learning experience. They should keep attention, illustrate a problem, or reward performance. Graphics should not bounce around the screen just for something to do.

IS THE SUBJECT MATTER PRESENTED IN A MODULAR DESIGN?

If the material is broken up into logically sequenced sections, the instructor can direct the student to a specific skill. This is particularly useful for adult education where there is a need to move quickly to that portion of the instructional content that suits the immediate need of the learner.

For example, a manager might wish to review a communications model which illustrates the barriers to understanding. The software should allow the student to move directly to this section of the material.

A modularly organized mathematics software package might be presented as follows:

Addition integers 1–4
Addition integers 5–9
Addition integers 10–20 with no carries
Addition integers 10–20 with carries

The instructor selects the lesson plan best suited to the student and the goals of the practice exercise.

Not only should the format and procedures be parallel and consistent from module to module, but also between programs. Once the student has learned a particular method for responding, for example, entering a number and pressing the *return* key, the next program should not require entering a letter and the *enter* key.

ARE THE INSTRUCTIONS APPROPRIATE?

The language level used for the instructions should match the level of the user. Using third-grade English to explain an addition exercise to first graders will require the teacher's assistance. Or using English to explain a lesson to bilingual workers may thwart their progress.

An effective way to avoid problems with instructions is to use *menus*. For example, a program that teaches metric measures might present the following menu:

Metric Measures
1. Volume
2. Linear
3. Weight
4. Metric measures table of conversions.
   Enter your choice and press *return* to continue.

The use of menus avoids lengthy explanations, delays, and errors. Multiple menus are used for further differentiation. For example if the student selected "Linear," the following menu might appear:

Metric Measures—Linear
1. Millimeters
2. Centimeters
3. Meters
4. Kilometers
5. Linear metric table of conversions
   Enter your choice and press *return* to continue.

If additional instructions are needed by the user a *help* routine is very useful. For example, let's say that the user doesn't know what *#2 Linear* means in the first menu above. While the menu appears on the screen, the user enters *HELP 2* and the following appears:

> Metric measures linear: Corresponds to inches, feet, yards, and miles. Includes millimeters, centimeters, meters, and kilometers. Press *return* to see menu.

If these detailed instructions appeared with each menu the student would be bored or slowed down. However, by making them accessible as needed, the user is not frustrated due to confusion or misunderstanding.

Too much information on the screen at one time discourages students. Breaking the information into blocks, using graphics, and using menus help to reduce information overload.

ARE THE RESPONSES SIMPLE?

The responses required by the software must also match the ability level of the user. It's best if the response is a single letter or digit. Other ways of responding are with a *light pen* pointing to the answer on the screen or with *joy sticks* or *game paddles* that move the *cursor* (bright moving dot) to a point on the screen indicating the location of the response. Entering words or sentences increases the opportunity for mistakes.

There should also be a provision for changing answers if the students accidentally press the wrong key or change their minds.

IS RESPONSE TIME VARIABLE?

The amount of time allowed for making a response also should correspond to difficulty level. Addition problems presented every 5 seconds with or without a response from the student denotes an expectation of rote memory proficiency level. Software that waits for a correct response before proceeding places less stress on the student. Some software prompts the student or presents the problem again when missed the first time. Others allow multiple tries or display the correct answer on the screen.

Good software allows the instructor to establish the pacing and number of problems presented to the individual learner. The instructor may even be able to add different items to the exercise, for example additional spelling words.

Some software will adjust the pacing and other difficulty factors based on the success rate of the student. Thus, if a student is getting all of the answers correct in less than 5 seconds and the pacing in every 10 seconds, the computer adjusts to a 5 second interval.

Adjusting the difficulty level to the individual promotes learning and avoids discouragement.

IS THE SOFTWARE EASY TO USE?

The manuals for the instructor should be well organized, referenced for quick access, and written in sufficient detail to be useful.

The instructions to the student should appear on the screen and should require almost no computer or keyboard knowledge or proficiency.

The keys inappropriate for the desired responses should be locked out. That is, if the menu requires a response of 1,2,3, or 4 followed by a *return,* and if it allows the use of the *delete* key to erase the answer, only those 6 keys should be allowed to send a signal to the microcomputer. Premature responses should also be locked out.

When this isn't done, people will accidentally or intentionally try another key and thus may lock up the system. Every time the system "crashes," the instructor must *reset* (start at the beginning) the program. If the software is tracking the individual's performance, all of this data could be lost with this type of interruption.

The instructions and illustrations on the screen should be clear and concise. They should give sufficient information to make the user feel comfortable with the software. There should be no more than one page of single-spaced instructions per program or the amount is overwhelming. A brief overview of the lesson at the beginning and then menu-driven instructions to select program parameters is preferred.

DOES THE SOFTWARE PROVIDE AN ADVANTAGE OVER A BOOK?

If the computer is used as a page turner for a book, it's being wasted. The special capabilities of the computer must be used to justify the expense.

For example, computer graphics are capable of illustrating the working relationships between mechanical parts. The user can assemble a model machine from pulleys, levers, chains, and gears. From this, the student observes the direction the pulleys and gears turn, the leverage the machine has to lift or move objects, the speeds at which the parts move, and the efficiency of the design.

No book or drawing on a page can illustrate the principles as well as the moving model on the screen. Computer modeling also saves money and time for buying and assembling materials to construct a mechanical model. Changes in the design on the screen are made quickly to test new configurations.

Another area where microcomputers aid in instruction is in financial modeling. With Financial Planning programs the student can vary company conditions such as income, advertising budget, inflation, taxes, and efficiency to determine the effect on the balance sheet. With the microcomputer's capabilities for performing rapid calculations, the answers appear in minutes allowing the student to try different strategies.

WILL THE SOFTWARE KEEP TRACK OF STUDENT PERFORMANCE AND PROGRESS?

The instructor needs to know at what difficulty level and proficiency level the student is performing. Also, the time the student requires to complete the lessons provides valuable information. Good software will create a record of right and wrong answers, number of prompts required, time to complete the assignment, and progress since the last exercise.

GOOD SOFTWARE MAY NOT BE ALL OF THE ABOVE

The likelihood that a particular software package will possess all of the desirable qualities is slim. However, if the instructors evaluate the software against these criteria, they will have a better understanding of the advantages and limitations. Such understanding could very well lead to a wiser purchase.

GLOSSARY

Cursor. The bright point or square on the screen that moves to indicate where the next entry or action will appear.

Documentation. All of the manuals for the user which tell how to operate the equipment and programs.

Game Paddles. Information input peripheral which moves the cursor on the screen.

Joy Stick. Information input peripheral which moves the cursor on the screen. Normally vertical, the lever can be tilted in any direction. Thus it allows the movement of the cursor to any position on the screen.

Light Pen. A photoelectric device which can detect the presence of light at a particular point on a screen. It looks like a pen and has a cable which connects it to a controller. When placed on the screen, the controller detects where the pen is located. Depending on the program, the computer will take appropriate action, for example, the selection of a response or the drawing of a character.

Menu. A list of choices presented by the software which represents a decision point in the running of the program.

Program. A sequential set of instructions that tells the computer what to do and when to do it.

Reset. To set the microcomputer to start at the beginning of the program.

Software. See *Program.*

16

PROGRAMMING IS
LIKE WRITING
A NOVEL

When a novelist begins a book, there are a number of things that must be done before a line of text is written. The writer must develop the plot, understand the characters, and describe the setting.

Writing a microcomputer program requires the same type of discipline. The plot of the program tells what is going to happen when. The data is manipulated and changed through the actions of the plot. The setting describes where the data is acted upon by the plot.

Like the novelist, the programmer must first create an outline. Otherwise, inconsistencies and lack of direction will plague the writer's efforts.

Program specifications outline what the program will do before any "dialog" or "action" takes place. This is perhaps the most important step in developing a system or program. If the plot is poor, the book will never sell.

There are two types of programs used on microcomputers. *Systems software* is the collective information which tells the computer how to communicate, how to relate to the *peripherals* (printer, terminal, etc.), and how to operate internally. *Applications software* is the instructions that tell the computer how to perform a specific function, for example, inventory control and payroll.

As a general rule it's best to purchase systems software. Where possible, applications software should also be purchased. Developing and *coding* (writing) good programs takes a great deal of skill and effort. However, there are circumstances that require customized programs. Also, there are times when modifying a purchased program makes it more efficient for a particular application. Besides, programming is fun!

BASIC STEPS TO GOOD PROGRAMMING

Eight basic steps are needed to produce a working program.

1. SELECT THE LANGUAGE. The reason different languages have been developed is to meet different needs. *FORTRAN* was developed to handle mathematical calculations. *COBOL* was developed to write business programs. *BASIC* was developed for multiple purpose use on microcomputers. Study the languages to determine the best one for the application.

2. LEARN THE LANGUAGE. Once the language is selected, the programmer must learn the language thoroughly. Efficiency in programming increases with experience, so don't be discouraged.

3. WRITE A DESCRIPTION OF THE DATA. Describe the types of data to be manipulated. For example, an inventory *record* might include such *fields* as part number, part name, and quantity on hand. List this information on a *record layout* (form) and describe what the acceptable values are for each *field* (data element). For example, if quantity on hand is a field, how many characters will it take to describe the maximum quantity? To what decimal place should the data be represented? If the maximum quantity in stock is 99, then two characters with no fraction (decimal) is needed to describe the field. Be sure to allow for growth. For example, if two characters are adequate now but three characters would work for the next ten years, build in the capacity for longer life.

4. DRAW A PICTURE OF THE ACTION. A playwright must move the actors around the stage. A programmer must design an *Input/Outut Flowchart* to show the movement of information around the computer hardware.

   A flow chart is a graphic representation of a system or a program which tells what will happen when and where. It's explicit, easily understood and organized. Every programmer should learn flowcharting at least to the extent of representing processes and decisions. The flowchart is a diagram of the plot telling what will happen, when, and where.

FIGURE 16-1. Record layout with field size.

```
RECORD FOR PARTS INVENTORY


PART NUMBER XXXXXX
PART NAME XXXXXXXXXXXXXX
LIST PRICE XXX.XX
COST XXX.XX
MOVEMENT CODE X
STANDARD PACKAGE XXX
MINIMUM STOCK XXXX
MAXIMUM STOCK XXXX
QUANTITY RECEIVED XXX
QUANTITY SHIPPED XXX
TRANSACTION DATE XX/XX/XX
BALANCE ON HAND XXXX
QUANTITY ON BACKORDER XXXX
SUPPLIER XXXXXXXXXXXXXX
ALTERNATE SUPPLIER XXXXXXXXXXXXXX
```

5. WRITE DETAILED INSTRUCTIONS IN ENGLISH. The program specifications tell in ordinary English what the program is about. All of the specifications should be developed before writing the coded program.

6. WRITE THE PROGRAM. Once the plot is defined, the setting described, and the characters developed, the action can begin. The action and dialog flows in sequential and logical steps until the conflict is resolved or the answer found. The instructions are coded in the selected language until a working program results.

7. DEBUG THE PROGRAM. Debugging is a troubleshooting process for removing errors from a program or system. The *interpretive* languages, for examples, BASIC, assist the programmer as the program is being written by presenting *error statements*. Compiled languages such as FORTRAN and COBOL tell the programmer where problems exist at the time the program is *compiled* (translated into a code the computer can understand).

8. FINALIZE THE DOCUMENTATION. The documentation consists of the data description (Step 2), the I/O flowcharts (Step 4), the program specifications (Step 5), and comment statements (*REM Statements* in BASIC, for example). Within the program itself, the programmer imbeds notes about what is happening. These statements do not affect the running of the program but serve as internal documentation for reference in *debugging* (editing) and modifying the program.

An operating manual should be written to define the complete procedure for loading the program, initializing the program for the day's run, using the functions of the system, and correcting errors during operation.

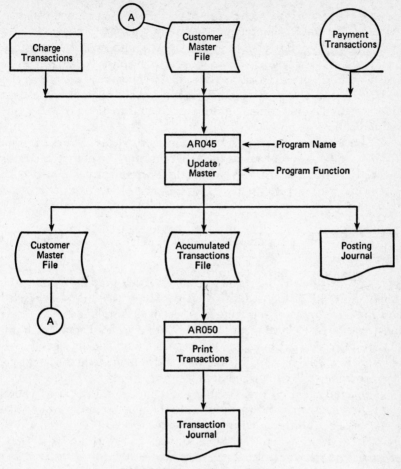

FIGURE 16–2. Input/Output flowchart.

PROGRAMMING TIPS

Map out the program statements into distinct functional segments (*subroutines*). For example, statements 100–300 are for the systems menu, 400–550 are for error checking, 500–1000 are for read/write routines, and 1000–2000 are for printing. Allow extra space for modifications and additions.

Program in simple, manageable pieces. Eighty percent of the total cost of large computer systems from design through maintenance is spent on maintenance. Developing the programs in functional segments makes troubleshooting and modifications much easier. For example, if all of the instructions for the operation of the menu are statements 100–300, changing the routine only involves looking at these instructions. Changes in an isolated routine will not affect something else in the program. This simplifies matters considerably. Studies show that a segment should not contain more than 60 instructions if it is to be maintainable.

Use a subroutine to check alpha/numeric fields. Errors in input lead to additional problems as the program runs. By putting the error check in a subroutine, it makes it easier for the programmer to invoke the subroutine wherever it's needed.

SUMMARY

Writing a program is like writing a novel. Much preparation must be done before the dialog and action starts. A language must be selected and mastered by the programmer. A detailed description of the data must be written for each record and field. A flowchart diagram is drawn to show the action steps in a logical, organized way. The detailed instructions are first written in English and then coded in the program language. The program is then debugged until it runs correctly.

Documentation is organized and developed to assist in operation and future maintenance. Programs are best written in distinct functional sections called subroutines. Error checks are needed to keep input errors from multiplying. When these steps are used, the program is efficient, effective, and maintainable.

GLOSSARY

Applications Software. Instructions that tell the computer how to perform a specific function, e.g., inventory control and payroll.

BASIC. An interpreted computer language used on most microcomputers.

COBOL. A compiled computer language used in business applications.

Coding. Writing a program to an established program language.

Compile. To translate a high-level programming language into machine code which the computer can understand.

Debug. To troubleshoot a program and correct errors.

Field. The individual factor in a record such as name, address, zip code, and telephone number.

FORTRAN. A computer language developed for scientific applications.

Input/Output Flowchart. A picture of the action in a program which shows the movement of information.

Logic Flowchart. A graphic representation of a system or a program that shows the operations occurring in the central processor.

Peripheral. A device attached to a microcomputer usually for input or output, e.g., printer, terminal, CRT, and keyboard.

Program Specifications. An outline of what the program will do which is written before any actual programming steps are written.

Record. A collection of fields.

Record Layout. A diagram of the fields and the space each field will occupy (number of digits), e.g., a field for telephone number may require 12 digits.

REM Statement. Remarks embedded in a BASIC program to make notations about what is happening; aids in debugging or modifying the program later. REM is short for *Remarks.*

Subroutine. A small portion of a program which performs a specific operation.

Systems Software. The collective information that tells the computer how to communicate, how to relate to the peripherals, and how to operate internally.

17

WHICH LANGUAGE IS BEST?

The user does not need to understand computer languages to operate a microcomputer. However, some familiarity with the advantages and disadvantages of using particular languages will help the buyer select the language best suited to the desired application.

Some hobbiests and business users want and need to program their computers. Custom-written programs are able to address needs too specialized for manufacturers to economically meet. Awkward operations in packaged programs can be modified and efficiency improved with a little programming modification. A word of caution, though. While modifications to manufacturer's programs can improve their function, altering the manufacturer's programs may void their warranty and infringe on copyrights.

A variety of languages have been developed to serve a number of application requirements. The characteristics of these languages determine the applications for which they are best suited. The "best" language provides efficient programming, computer operation, and trouble-shooting capabilities.

LOW-LEVEL LANGUAGE

To the user *machine* and *assembly languages* are relics of the past. *Machine code* actually addresses the electronic structure of the computer and requires no interpretation. It's the only language the computer really understands and can use. An assembler is the next step. Assembler language programming is programming at the very edge of the computer machine language. For this reason assembler language programs run very fast.

Because the instructions are written in minute detail (*low-level language*) and are specific to the particular machine, the programmer must be skilled and patient. Assembler language programming is time-consuming and prone to error. The advantages, however, are faster operating speeds and the ability to perform highly technical operations not otherwise possible. Many word processors, high-speed games, and data-management programs are written in assembly language. It is hundreds of times faster than an interpretive language and many times faster than a compiled program.

HIGH-LEVEL LANGUAGE

High-level languages resemble English. Unfortunately, the microcomputer cannot yet understand conversational English. The robots pictured in the science fiction movies and television programs are no doubt possible, however developing this level of sophistication is many years away.

High-level languages are easier to use than low ones. The programmer need not be as skilled as those using low-level languages and the opportunity for error is reduced because the *compiler* (translating program) warns the programmer of *syntax* (grammatical) and suspected logic errors.

BASIC is the most common high-level microcomputer language. However, since the computer must translate the language into machine code as it executes the instructions, BASIC tends to operate slowly. Machine code is understood by the computer. BASIC is called an *interpreted* language because it must be translated each time the program is run. Recently, compiler versions of BASIC have emerged which have eliminated many objections to the use of this important language.

There are two methods to translate high-level languages into machine language—a *compiler* and an *interpreter*.

A *compiler* translates (compiles) the entire high-level program into machine code before execution begins. The user must request execution separately. The output from a compiler is a *load module* (new program written in computer executable form) which is stored on disk for use at execution time. Once a program is *compiled* (translated) and working properly, it doesn't have to be recompiled. Since compiled programs don't have to be interpreted during each execution, they run very fast.

Another advantage to compilers is that after the program is compiled, the compiler program itself is no longer needed and thus no longer takes up valuable room in RAM. This leaves more memory for the program when it executes.

Compilers inform the programmer of errors at compile time. The programmer then makes the necessary modifications and recompiles the entire program. Even though this adds to trouble-shooting and development time, it pays off at execution time when the program is correct and no longer has to be recompiled.

Interpreters function as on-line (immediate) error checking programs. The interpreter is retained in memory while the program is being written and executed. As the programmer enters a line of code, it is immediately checked for errors. If incorrect, a message is given to the user and the programmer corrects the problem before continuing. However, since the interpreter must translate the high level language each time the program is run, computer execution slows down.

Interpreters such as BASIC are very popular on microcomputers.

When selecting hardware and software, the user should consider the differences in these translating methods. For example, COBOL, FORTRAN, and Pascal are generally considered compiled languages. BASIC and APL are interpretive languages. More about that later.

TIPS FOR BUYING A LANGUAGE

The language should be compatible with the computer. Some languages require large amounts of internal memory. Others may not be available for certain brands of computers. Review what is available for the computer and its memory restrictions.

The memory capacity of the computer determines if a compiled or interpretive language is appropriate. Since high-level compilers generally require large memory capacity, interpretive languages are more common for microcomputers.

The language should suit the application and the computer. Each language has strengths and weaknesses. For example, FORTRAN was developed for engineering and mathematical applications which require the manipulation of complex formulas. COBOL was developed for business applications and LOGO for educational use.

The language should be easy to learn. Most business users and hobbiests don't want to master a complex, detailed language such as *assembler*. The easier the language is to use, the more likely the user will gain full benefit from the computer. As a general rule, programs written in high-level languages are easier to write and to maintain.

WHICH ONE TO BUY?

The reasons for selecting a particular language vary from personal preference to highly technical justification. Some of the qualities of the more popular microcomputer languages appear below:

1. BASIC (Beginners All-purpose Symbolic Instructional Code) is relatively compact, uses standard English words, and is easy to learn. It has special features for graphics and file handling. In addition, BASIC is an interpreted language which makes program development and testing easier. BASIC is the dominant language for microcomputer, even though it's slow in execution and doesn't have the luxury of the memory required to give good descriptive error messages.
2. FORTRAN (FORmula TRANslation) was developed for conversion of mathematical formulas into machine code. This is one of the first computer languages developed and typically runs very fast.
3. COBOL (COmmon Business Oriented Language) requires large amounts of memory to compile, but gives good error diagnostics. Most microcomputer memories cannot accommodate COBOL. The language is especially useful for business applications and is closer to conversational English than most other languages. COBOL is a verbose compiled language.
4. *Pascal* is modular in structure and forces the programmer into good writing habits. This makes it easier for the user to find and resolve errors. Pascal has an intermediate stage called *P-code* which can be translated to fit most any computer.

    Because Pascal can be used on numerous computers, it has become very popular. Once a system is written in Pascal, it is easily convertible (via P-code translation) to other machines. This flexibility is referred to as *portability*.

5. APL is simple, compact, interpretive, and easy to learn. Used primarily for applications requiring numerous mathematical operations; particularly adapted to handling large arrays (matrices). However, it doesn't lend itself to general use and doesn't handle high volumes of data well.

7. LISP and SNOBOL manipulate non-numerical data very efficiently. They are especially adaptable to information retrieval, pattern generation, algebraic manipulation, and linguistic analysis.

8. COGO (COordinate GeOmetry), STRESS (STRuctural Engineering Systems Solver), and ICES (Integrated Civil Engineering Systems) are special problem-oriented languages that lack flexibility outside their intended use. Very few of these languages are available for microcomputers, and they are limited in application.

9. LOGO is a computer language which allows learning through exploration, trial and error, and discovery. Using this English-type language, the students correct problems and debug programs. There are no right or wrong answers. LOGO incorporates the learning-without-teaching philosophy of education. The students create geometric figures and animated movies. They assign shapes, colors, speed and direction to objects, and experiment with lines and proportions.

WHICH LANGUAGE IS "BEST?"

The user should select the programming language that best matches the requirements of the application and the operating system.

Low-level languages (machine and assembly) are fast, but they require a great deal of programmer skill and patience.

High-level languages (COBOL, Pascal, and BASIC) are easier to use. Since they require compilers or interpreters to convert them to machine code, their execution is slower than with low-level languages. Since one instruction in a high-level language translates into many machine code instructions, high-level languages serve as a shorthand to computer programming. The resemblance of high-level languages to English makes them easier to write and easier to debug (troubleshoot).

The language should be suited to the application, be compatible with the computer and it's memory capacity, and be easy to learn and maintain.

GLOSSARY

Assembly Language. A low-level computer language that uses symbols to represent machine language instructions. It's much more readable and efficient than machine language.

APL. A simple, compact, interpretive, and easy to learn language. However, it doesn't lend itself to general use and doesn't handle high volumes of data well.

BASIC (Beginners All-purpose Symbolic Instructional Code). A compact computer language which uses standard English words that make it easy to learn. An interpreted language which is dominant in the microcomputer industry.

COBOL (COmmon Business Oriented Language). A compiled language which requires large amounts of memory. Most microcomputers cannot accommodate COBOL since it is verbose.

COGO (COordinate GeOmetry). Special problem-oriented language.

Compiler. A program that translates (compiles) the high-level program into machine code.

Debug. To troubleshoot and correct a program.

FORTRAN (FORmula TRANslation). A language developed for conversion of mathematical formulas into machine code. Runs very fast.

High-Level Language. A computer language which resembles English and needs a compiler or interpreter to translate the program into machine code which the computer can use.

ICES (Integrated Civil Engineering System). Special problem-oriented language.

Interpreter. An on-line (immediate) error checking program retained in memory (RAM) while the program is being written and executed. Since the interpreter translates the high-level language, e.g. BASIC, each time the program is run, computer execution is slow.

LISP. A language that manipulates non-numerical data efficiently.

Load Module. The output from a compiler. A compiled program is in computer executable form.

LOGO. A language especially adaptable to learning that follows advanced learning theories.

Low-Level Language. Machine code and assembly languages which are written in minute detail. They have faster operating speeds but require greater programming skill and patience and are machine-dependent (specific to a particular computer).

Machine Code. A language that actually addresses the electronic structure of the computer and requires no interpretation. The machine-executable version of a program.

Pascal. A modular, high-level language which can be used on many different microcomputers.

RAM (Random-Access Memory). The erasable memory in a computer which can be very rapidly accessed by the CPU.

SNOBOL. A language that manipulates non-numerical data efficiently.

STRESS (STRuctural Engineering Systems Solver). A special problem-oriented language.

Syntax. The rules which describe how programming language statements must be constructed, i.e., the grammer of the language.

18

IS SECURITY REALLY A PROBLEM?

Bill Masters prided himself on his ability to write and sell interesting and challenging game programs. The youngsters in the neighborhood flocked to his house after school to try out his newest creations. While Bill was at work one day, his house burned to the ground. He lost his computer, but worse, he lost all of his game programs. Two years of effort and thousands of dollars went up in smoke.

Al Williams installed a system in his lawnmower repair business. He spent 18 months developing special programs that would keep track of customer work tickets and parts inventories. A disgruntled employee entered "four-letter words" throughout the customer data file and altered some of the programs. His computer was down several weeks and he spent hundreds of frustrating hours trying to find and solve the programming problems.

It took a medical supply company months to detect that an employee was using the computer to ship supplies to phony accounts. They lost thousands of dollars of inventory and spent weeks auditing the system to find and correct the information.

There are a number of precautions a microcomputer owner can use to protect data, programs, and money. Since no one is immune to disaster, the extra effort is worth it.

WHO CAN USE THE COMPUTER?

Small children are potentially hazardous to the health of any computer system. Physical security starts with locked cabinets, closets, and doors. The best security against a toddler is making the equipment and files inaccessible. One home computer owner keeps his micro in a large walk-in closet. During the day while he's at work, the closet door is latched to prevent entry.

Older children can abide by a strict set of rules. If they are allowed use of the computer, their tapes or diskettes should be stored in their own box.

PROMPTED PROGRAMS ARE ROADMAPS TO DISASTER

Some programs are so easy to use that youngsters should not be allowed access to them. *Prompted programs* can make program alteration or data entry easy. Prompting tells the user step-by-step how to operate the program. A few accidental or intentional entries can cause weeks of rework. Some users keep their diskettes in locked cabinets.

BACK-UP IS ESSENTIAL

Backing up (copying) programs and data should be a routine procedure for every computer user. Even the home computer is vulnerable to fire, electrical aberrations in the power lines, and mechanical failure. Any one of these can ruin in seconds information stored on tapes and diskettes.

There should be a back-up copy available where the computer is being used and another at an off-site location.

Peggy Ryan used her computer for word processing. She stored her articles and book chapters two places on the same disk. This way, if she ruined one file, she could call in the back-up file to continue. Every few hours she would transfer the data from the disk to a back-up disk which she kept in a box near the computer. Every day or so Peggy would make a copy of the disk and take it across the street to her friend's house. This off-site copy protected her from losing the manuscript to catastrophe.

One day Peggy had worked all morning revising some chapters of her book to present to an editor. A power failure occurred and the data on her working disk was lost. Her back-up disk saved her hours of work. Now she backs up her articles because she wants to, not because she "should."

Similar precautions should be taken by the business computer user.

The frequency for backing up information depends on the type and the amount of use. If entering the information is time-consuming or if the information is difficult to retrieve or duplicate, backing up might be done at the end of each operation. Some businesses back up their information on-site daily and off-site weekly. One company backs up the monthly accounts receivable file after statements are produced. The user must decide the frequency that provides the optimal protection for the effort required.

SECURITY IN A BUSINESS

The office computer environment is more difficult to control. Not only must the data be protected from physical loss, but in some instances, the confidentiality of information must be preserved. Critical functions like writing checks or printing shipping orders must have controls which will deter fraud or detect discrepancies. With positive management planning, the risk of loss and theft can be reduced considerably.

Selective Training is Best

An employee who doesn't know how to use the computer can't deliberately alter its function. Some companies go out of their way to orient and train every employee on the complete use of the computer. After all, it is the new "toy" and owners are proud of the capabilities and their own proficiency.

If possible, however, employees should only know the part of a system necessary to do their own job. For example, the person who enters payroll data should not be able to print paychecks. The person who prints paychecks should not have access to the blank checks stored in a locked cabinet. The person who prints checks should not be responsible for signing them. This type of security is called *segregation of duties.* Segregation of duties between the computer functions and manual procedures helps to provide the checks and balances that avoid fraud.

Passwords Are Not a Panacea

A *password* is a special word or code that must be entered into the terminal before the process will run. Passwords are used to prevent nonauthorized personnel from accidentally or intentionally having access to program alteration, data entry, or to confidential information.

Do Not Use Initials for Passwords

Initials are too obvious a choice for a password and serve little purpose. A less familiar code such as the last four digits of a social security number, a telephone number backwards, a zip code backwards, or a random number is a better choice.

A good system does not display the password on the monitor as the operator enters it. This prevents observers from seeing the code easily.

Passwords will slow down novices. However, they will not stop someone with malicious intent.

Controls and Accountability

The best protection against alteration and fraud is being able to trace who is responsible. Employees aware of their accountability will think twice before making changes. If only one person has the key to the cabinet retaining blank checks, that person is implicated if extra checks are printed. If only one person knows how to create shipping papers, the field of suspects is limited when phony shipments are discovered.

Logs are also useful tools for tracing problems. Employees using the computer should enter their name, date, time, program used, and purpose. Then, if there is a problem the next time the accounts receivable program is used, the user log will indicate who executed it last.

A major accounting firm keeps its microcomputer in a locked room. The keeper of the log has the key. This provides additional protection for the equipment and systems.

Manual checks of input and output will detect discrepancies. For example, someone should be responsible for inspecting the listing of orders shipped to see if the quantities and prices make sense. Payroll totals should be balanced and periodically examined to insure that discrepancies don't go unnoticed. The manual reviews should be done by someone not involved in the computer operation. The business owner should determine what manual procedures are necessary and should establish procedures that are followed regularly.

What Happens When It Fails?

Management should have contingency plans for handling computer functions if the computer *goes down* (breaks or ceases to function). Failure can result from program alteration, from tampered data, untrained operators, equipment failure, or power outage.

Manual procedures should be designed and tested for order processing, payroll, accounts payable and receivable, inventory management, or other critical processes in case the computer goes out of commission. Data should continue to be accumulated during the repair time. When the computer is working again, the records can be brought up-to-date with a minimum of interruption and duplication of effort.

Anyone can "beat the system," no matter how elaborate the security. Elaborate security systems are cumbersome to maintain and expensive. The selection of reliable employees is important. Only trustworthy people should be given access to the computer.

GLOSSARY

Back-Up. Copies of disks, tapes, or paper reports that can be stored onsite or off and preferably both.

Go Down. A slang term meaning to stop functioning.

Log. A written ledger that indicates who uses the computer, when, and how.

Password. A special word or code that must be keyed into the system before the process will run.

Program. The step-by-step instructions that tell the computer what to do.

Prompt (Prompted Program). A character or message printed by the program to signal the operator what action is required to continue.

Segregation of Duties. A security precaution that separates the duties of people using a system in such a way that no one person can perform the entire process, such as creating paychecks, or applying cash to accounts receivable.

19

SOFTWARE FROM ABORT TO VIRTUAL MEMORY

Some computer buffs and serious users want to know more about the software (systems and programs) than the typical user. For those who have a need for in-depth information, this chapter is a glossary of software terms not found elsewhere in this book.

GLOSSARY OF SOFTWARE TERMS

Abort. To terminate. Usually because of a malfunction, a program will automatically or, at the request of the computer operator, cease functioning.

Array. A set of variables which may be arranged within a logical relationship; a table or matrix of data.

Boot (Bootstrap). A set of resident instructions usually found in ROM which can be initiated by a manual switch. The instructions tell the computer what to do to start up the hardware.

Branch Instruction. An instruction which causes the processor to jump to another location in the program, that is, to break the normal numerical instruction sequence.

Endless Loop. A process which occurs when a branch instrument sends the processor to an earlier statement and causes the routine (portion of the program) to recycle continuously.

Executive Program. A program that controls or supervises the execution of other programs or the overall operation of a system.

Exit. To leave one program for another.

Initialize. To reset a system to its starting condition; to set various parts of a program so it will behave the same way each time it is repeated. Initializing a disk removes flaws in the disk and prepares the disk for use by the computer.

Key. A retrieval code contained in a record, for example, the surname is a key field in a telephone directory.

Label. Descriptive identifier; group of characters used to describe a file, message, or record.

Line Number. Certain programming languages such as FORTRAN and BASIC require that the programmer assign a particular line number at the start of each instruction. The program is then executed in numerical sequence.

Loop. A group of instructions in a program that can be executed more than once before the program continues, for example an incremental counter (keep adding 1 each time this loop is run until the counter reaches 65 and then continue with the program).

Null. Program instruction meaning to do nothing. Nulls allow time to pass between processing instructions.

Object Code. A computer language written by an interpreter or compiler from high-level language; the code the processor can understand.

Patch. To temporarily modify the software.

PEEK. In the BASIC language a command which allows the user to read a specified memory address.

POKE. In the BASIC language a command which allows the user to write a piece of information into a specified memory address.

Reset. See *Initialize.*

Run. To execute one or more programs.

Screen Clear. To erase all data from the CRT.

Sort Key. The field used to sort records, for example the surname in a telephone directory.

Source Code. Program written by a human programmer usually in a high-level language.

String. A sequence of records, words, or characters usually in a specific order.

String Variable. A character string treated as a single grouping of characters. For example, in word processing the program is able to search for "rd pro" instead of "*word*" or "*pro*cessor" even though it's not a distinct English word.

Swapping. A process for reading in only a portion of a program from secondary storage and putting it back on the disk when the next segment is required to continue. This process saves space in RAM. See *Virtual Memory.*

Syntax. Rules which decide how the program language is constructed; grammatical rules and definitions of terms.

Trap. A method for finding program errors.

Unconditional Branch. A jump in the program instructions which is always executed.

Verification. A method for checking input data to make sure it is entered correctly. For example, a check to see if the data is entered as alpha or numeric characters. See *Editing.*

Virtual Memory. An operating system technique which automatically transfers program sections or data between the disk and main memory; a method for increasing the effective memory capacity of the computer. See *Swapping.*

V

WHICH ONE IS BEST?

20

PERFORMING THE NEEDS ANALYSIS

When a small business, professional practice, or job function rapidly grows, it becomes more and more difficult for management to control records on customers, inventory, sales performance, scheduling, and profits. Microcomputers have made it economically possible to achieve these goals.

However, before software (programs) and hardware (equipment) is selected, the computer buyer must determine what functions are causing bottlenecks, inefficiencies, and excessive costs to the business. By conducting a *needs analysis* (a study of the manual systems and procedures) the buyer determines what needs the microcomputer can address.

PROBLEMS OR SYMPTOMS?

Identifying the problems requires distinguishing between problems and their symptoms. Some questions to ask are:

Are procedures defective or overly expensive?
Is there inadequate or too much control?
Who is affected?
Are the machines wrong?

An equipment repair company applied these questions to their operation and came up with these observations:

One aggravation to the business was answering telephone inquiries about whether the customer's repair was complete. Often when customers called, parts customers were left waiting at the counter or equipment sales presentations were interrupted. It took from two to ten minutes to determine the exact status of a repair ticket. The process was inefficient, time-consuming, nonproductive, and costly.

SOMETIMES A COMPUTER IS THE ANSWER

Sometimes the answers lie in altering poor practices and procedures, not in adding a computer. However, if the procedures are adequate and the implementation is done well, and there are still bottlenecks, excessive overtime, and unmet deadlines, a microcomputer may be the answer.

The equipment service company decided that a microcomputer could relieve their information retrieval problems. They purchased a microcomputer and installed a customer status file which could be sorted by ticket number or customer name. Thus, if the customer did not have the ticket number when they called, the record could still be found.

The computer didn't reduce the total workload but allowed the sales clerk to spread out the work so overload and poor service didn't occur at peak periods. The change of status entries were made at slow periods and the rapid information access was available during busy business hours. The job became less of a hassle and customers were pleased with the organization.

DEFINE OBJECTIVES

The next process in performing the needs analysis is to define the objectives of buying a computer. What are the goals? Faster or smoother operations, a better end product, lower costs? Write formal descriptions of the "outputs" or end products and define the problem in detail.

The service company had several goals for the computer: 1) to provide fast information retrieval on customer status; 2) to reduce the hassle to the sales clerk from telephone inquiries on customer work status; 3) to improve customer service during peak loads; and 4) to control work flow more efficiently.

STUDY THE CURRENT SYSTEM

Make a plan for studying the manual system currently being used. What are the objectives of the study? The methods? The time schedule? The

FIGURE 20–1. Logic flowchart.

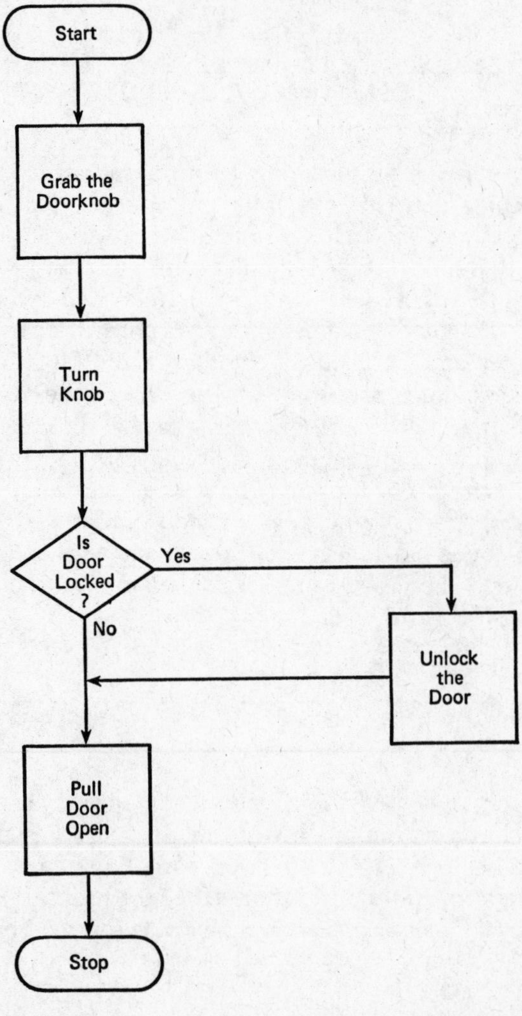

FIGURE 20–2. Flowchart symbols.

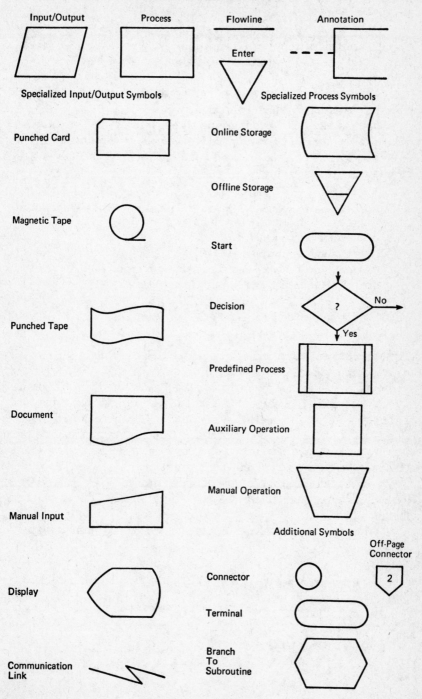

funds and personnel? The personality problems? And, what is the plan of action?

Once the plan for the study is crystallized, the fact gathering begins. The needs analysis requires information on the organization, procedures, forms, volume of work (peak loads), individual work loads (balance), machines used, and office or plant layout.

After the information is gathered, flowcharts should be developed showing how the information and paper flows.

Analyze the facts to determine where improvement is possible. What procedures can be eliminated, combined, or simplified? Are the sequences for the procedures logical and efficient? When analyzing the facts look for the following:

> Organizational weakness or practices; lack of proper delegation; inadequate control; defective communication.
> How peak loads are handled.
> Uneven workload distribution.
> Equipment performance—condition, quality, adequacy.
> Layout for production and transportation efficiency.
> Defective procedures.
> Forms control and design.

The service company also had problems with controlling their repair parts inventory levels and ordering procedures. Shop inefficiencies were attributed to inadequate inventory levels and slow ordering procedures.

For several years the company had maintained a perpetual card inventory control system. However, the clerical time required to post invoices and packing slips to the cards became too expensive and were not cost justifiable. A parts order log organized by supplier worked well. However, back orders were difficult to track.

The analysis of the current system determined that the procedures were as effective as possible given the clerical time available to perform the functions.

When analyzing procedures, repeatedly ask the question "Why?" For example,

> What is being done? Why?
> Where is it done? Why?
> When is it done? Why?
> Who does it? Why?
> How is it done? Why?

What was being done by the service company? The order book was being kept, but the perpetual inventory system had been dropped. Why? Because a procedure for ordering parts was critical and the inventory control system was so expensive to maintain, it couldn't be cost justified.

Where? At the front counter. Why? Because the sales clerk who was responsible was stationed at that location.

When? When the workload was light. Why? Because that was the only time available to place orders.

Who? The sales clerk. Why? The person who was in charge of selling parts over the counter, receiving parts shipments and pricing work tickets would have the best knowledge of parts needs and levels.

How? By posting parts in an order notebook organized by supplier? Why? To keep track of orders already placed, to avoid duplication of orders, and to know what to do with the parts when they arrived. Some parts were placed in stock and others were given to a mechanic to complete the work. Also the order book served as a control to be sure that suppliers were shipping the parts ordered.

The solutions to the identified problems must be practical. They must be simple for the employees to understand and easy to follow. The new procedures should be permanent, workable, and cost justifiable. The employees make procedures work so the new operations should be seen as a major improvement.

THE MICROCOMPUTER SOLUTION

If the solution is a microcomputer, the next step is to find software which will perform the needed functions. Determine what job the applications software is to perform. Is the software compatible with the computer? And is the software efficient?

If there is no software available, contact a professional systems analyst for advice and customized programming. Custom-designed programs are expensive and take time to develop and debug (troubleshoot). If prepackaged programs will do most of the job, consider them first.

The service company could not find a customer information retrieval program that would serve their needs. Since this type of data base system (file) was relatively straightforward, they hired a programmer to write a customized program. The inventory control problem was more common to business applications and thus a program was available from the computer software manufacturer.

The computer and new procedures surrounding its arrival should not be a surprise. From the earliest point possible, employees should be involved in solving the problems. Employees usually can help identify the problems and set objectives and expectations for the changes. Their involvement throughout the process relieves employee anxieties and fears. They will see how the computer will benefit the company and what will happen to their jobs. Enlisting their cooperation and asking for ideas builds pride of authorship within the employees.

Prior to installing the equipment and procedures a plan should be developed for converting to the system. Develop plans for programming, testing, installing, converting to new procedures, printing new forms, remodeling, and training personnel.

Determine if the whole system will begin at once or if it will be installed in stages. Decide which manual systems should run parallel until the automated system is proven. A well-thought-out plan minimizes difficulties and frustrations.

The service company installed the customer information retrieval system first. This was quickly accomplished since only 50–60 records had to be created. Everyone benefited from the relief to the sales clerk, especially the customers. The employees became familiar with the operation of the terminal and programs.

Everyone looked forward to the installation of the order and inventory control systems. These would take longer since nearly 5,000 parts records had to be created and current inventory taken. By the time the parts control system was ready to go on-line, the sales clerk was efficient at entering data on the terminal.

After any new system is installed, manual or automated, there are faults to correct. Managers and supervisors need to check to see if procedures are followed and if results and objectives are met. Modifications and additional training may be required before the computer system runs smoothly.

For example, the service company found that the data entry program on the customer file was cumbersome. The sequence for entering the information did not correspond to the sequence in which the data appeared on the work ticket. Resequencing the order in which the fields appeared on the screen (customer name, address . . .) to match the work order made data entry more efficient and accurate.

IS IT WORTH THE TROUBLE?

To some people these steps seem cumbersome and time-consuming. However, followed in spirit, if not to the letter, the selection, purchase, installation, and performance of a microcomputer will be a positive experience.

GLOSSARY

Data Base. A large file of organized data which users draw upon for a common pool of up-to-date information (central files).

Debug. To troubleshoot a program for the purpose of correcting errors in logic.

Fields. Factors in a record such as name, address, zip code, telephone, etc.

Flowchart. A graphic representation of facts, arrangements, or processes; a picture of a procedure or method.

Needs Analysis. A study of the manual systems and procedures.

Hardware. The equipment associated with the computer system, e.g., printer, disk drive unit, and microprocessor.

Record. A combination of fields which completely describes one unit in a file. For example, an inventory card for one part contains all of the field information for one part, i.e., part number, description, price, quantity on hand.

Software. The computer instructions that tell the system what to do and how to do it.

21

PUTTING IT
ALL TOGETHER

DO YOU NEED A MICROCOMPUTER?

A computer is needed when control and time management becomes difficult or impossible. The mistake many people make is going to their local computer store or discount chain and buying equipment first. The next morning they find out the equipment works but the computer does not do what they want.

Home users buy microcomputers for entertainment, word processing, skill development, home environment control, and for communicating with large computers at the bank, library, and courthouse.

Business and professional people use microcomputers to access information on customers, inventory, sales performance, scheduling, and profits. Timely performance feedback is essential for continued growth and profitability.

Educators and trainers use microcomputers for conducting practice drills, for scoring tests and keeping student records, for teaching computer literacy courses, for developing management decision-making capabilities, and for studying computerized models of mechanical devices.

To avoid buying the wrong computer system, shop for the software first. Select the programs that provide the services and information needed. It's what the computer does that is important, not how much memory it has or the number and size of its disk drives. Finding the prewritten programs that do the job is the first and most difficult task.

SOFTWARE ISN'T SO HARD

Software is the instructions that tell the computer what to do and how to do it. Good software makes a computer of moderate quality work well. Poor software makes a sophisticated microcomputer inoperative.

Applications software tells the computer how to do inventory, how to play the game, or how to conduct the course. *Systems software* tells the computer how to operate, for example, how to communicate with the disk drive unit, the printer, and the terminal. Systems software also provides common tasks such as sorting, file copying, and other important routines.

DON'T WRITE THAT PROGRAM

Writing programs is a difficult and lengthy process. Most businesspeople and educators don't have the time or financial resources to create their own programs. However, the home user may wish to "play" with the computer and thus will often learn to program as a hobby.

First find out if a commercial package is available to do the job. Get names from the dealer of customers who use the system and call them. Also, see a demonstration. Set up a test with live or real data. Be sure to read the manuals to see if you can understand them. There should be manuals for operating the machine and separate manuals for each software package.

Don't try to find a system that does everything. If the software relieves the bottlenecks and drudgery of the current procedures, the computer will pay for itself.

Hardware refers to the microcomputer equipment. The computer itself is a piece of hardware. The *terminal* (keyboard and monitor), the *secondary memory storage device* (cassette tape recorder/player or disk drive unit), and other attachments are referred to as hardware.

The *input peripherals* bring information to the computer. These include the keyboard, cassette tape player, disk drive unit, light pen, joy stick, game paddles, and sensors such as thermometers and intruder detection devices.

The *output peripherals* receive information from the computer. These include the Cathode Ray Tube (CRT) or TV-type screen, the printer, the cassette tape recorder, disk drive unit, and controllers such as valves and thermostats.

Large amounts of information are *loaded* (entered) into the computer from cassette tapes or floppy disks. Secondary storage devices will also store large amounts of information sent from the computer.

Cassette tapes are similar to those on which music is recorded. *Floppy disks* are flexible records made from material similar to magnetic tape. The *disk drive* reads the information on the spinning disk and transfers it to the computer where it is processed.

THE TERMINAL DECISION

The *terminal* (CRT) image should be easy to read and the keyboard should have a light and positive touch. The display on the TV-type screen should be clear enough to read for long periods of time. CRT monitors are more legible than a modified television receiver. However, many home users prefer the savings found with the black and white television.

Some questions to ask about monitors are:

How clear are the characters?
How many characters per line are displayed?
Does the monitor have color capabilities?
Is a speaker available for audio output?
Is the screen tinted green for eye comfort?
What size is the picture?
Are the controls accessible?

If the user wants to display reports on the monitor, the screen must have the capability of producing the number of characters per line in the report. Eighty characters per line is a common width.

Like an expensive typewriter keyboard, the keys should be comfortably paced and the touch should be positive but not tiring. A ten-key numerical pad increases input speeds and improves the accuracy of entering numerical data.

Word processing applications such as writing articles and correspondence require upper- and lower-case letters. The monitor should be able to display both.

The terminal must match the application. Business reports look fine in black and white. However, Star Invaders would not be the same without color.

SECONDARY MEMORY

Many applications require the use of floppy disks for extended memory. Cassette tapes are fine for loading games and for disk back-up. However, they are too slow and unreliable for business use.

TIPS FOR BUYING A PRINTER

Printers are evaluated on print quality, paper feed, paper size and type, interfaces (to the computer), noise level, printing speed, size and weight, special printing abilities, durability and service, and price.

As print quality and speed increase, so does the price. Sometimes compromises must be made in requirements. *Dot matrix* printers are useful for most business applications. This type of printer creates a character by printing tiny dots to create the image. However, original correspondence with word processing requires a letter-quality printer.

Above all, the printer must be compatible with the computer. If the *interface* or electrical connections and signals aren't compatible, the printer should not be purchased. Have the dealer demonstrate the computer and the printer operating together.

EVALUATING DOCUMENTATION

The quality of the equipment and documentation is critical for training, implementation, and systems design. If the manuals are poor, initial start-up and maintenance will be time-consuming and expensive.

Microcomputer dealers cannot afford to give extensive, free start-up support. Therefore, the user must be able to rely on the documentation and *menu driven* (prompted) programs to make the system operational.

The *systems manual* describes how the entire system works. The *users manual* tells what information must be entered, how output reports are formated, and what a particular function will do. The *operators manual* tells the user how to run the equipment and programs.

To evaluate the quality of the manuals ask the following questions:

What language ability is needed by the user to read the manuals?
What computer expertise is assumed by the manuals?
Are the manuals organized and easy to search?
Do summary lists give quick instructions and definitions?
Are the illustrations clear and helpful?
Is the information relevant to the application?
Do the manuals give you indigestion?

The quality of the documentation is next in importance to the quality of the programs themselves. And yet, reviewing the documentation is frequently overlooked.

VENDOR SUPPORT

What will the dealer do for the buyer after the sale? In many cases, the buyer should expect very little assistance. Some questions that should be addressed before the sale are:

Will the dealer provide training?
Will the dealer service the equipment under warranty?
Does the dealer stock service parts? Supplies?
Will the dealer repair the unit on site?
Is a loaner available during repairs?

Ask for a list of customers and call them to check out their experience with the dealer.

SUMMARY

Microcomputers have made it financially possible for small business owners, professionals, and managers to get timely information on business performance. Educators can use microcomputers to aid instruction and to relieve their administrative record keeping. Home computers provide many hours of pleasure and facilitate the management of leisure time.

Because the microcomputer industry is new and growing, the buyer must take the responsibility for the selection and start-up of a microcomputer operation. Evaluate the software, hardware, documentation, and dealer support before buying. See demonstrations and check dealer references. With these precautions and preparation, the likelihood of success will be greater.

GLOSSARY

Application Software. Instructions that tell the computer how to perform a specific function, e.g. payroll and accounts receivable.

Cassette (Recorder/Player). A tape recorder/player and magnetic tape cartridge used to input information into or record output information from the microcomputer.

CPU (Central Processing Unit). The "brain" of the microcomputer that performs the arithmetic and logic functions. The CPU controls all computer functions, operates peripheral devices, and controls access to memory.

CRT (Cathode Ray Tube). A peripheral device resembling a television that displays input and output information to the operator.

Disk Drive Unit. A peripheral device that spins a floppy or hard disk and reads information from and writes information to the secondary storage.

Dot Matrix. A printing style which uses small dots to form the characters. The results are similar to newspaper print.

Floppy Disk (Diskette). A flexible record made of magnetic tapelike material used to store data in secondary storage.

Hardware. The equipment or electrical components of a microcomputer.

Input Peripheral. A device that enters data into the computer, e.g., keyboard, terminal, ten-key pad.

Interface. An electrical device that connects an input or output peripheral to the computer.

Keyboard. A typewriter type of device used to enter information into the computer.

Load. To transfer information from storage into internal memory or transfer from the memory to secondary storage.

Output Peripheral. A device that reads data from the computer, e.g., printer, CRT, disk drive unit.

Printer. A typewriter-type device that makes a printed copy of the data, programs, or communications from the CPU. It usually does not have a keyboard of its own.

Systems Manual. The manual that describes how an entire system works. The overview or umbrella for the other manuals.

Systems Software. The information that tells the computer in sequential steps how to communicate, how to relate to the peripherals, and how to operate internally.

Terminal. The combination of keyboard and CRT or television monitor.

Users Manual. The manual that tells what information must be entered, how output reports are formated, and what a particular program will do.

GLOSSARY

Abort. To terminate processing. Usually, because of a malfunction, a program will automatically or at the request of the computer operator cease functioning.

Access Time. The time it takes for the computer to read or write information.

Accumulator. Another term for register. A dedicated storage location within the CPU. The more accumulators a microcomputer has, the more arithmetic or logic operations that can be carried out simultanenously.

Address. A way of referencing a memory location, that is, identifying it.

Addressing. The process of accessing a specific memory location.

ALU (Arithmetic Logic Unit). The part of the microprocessor which performs arithmetical and logic operations. For example, *add, subtract, multiply* and *divide* are arithmetic functions while *and, or, not* are logic operations.

Analogue. A type of computer which does not work by detecting an "on" or "off" state (1 or 0 in binary code) but works with continuous states such as voltage changes. Often used in equipment control and scientific applications.

ANSI (American National Standards Institute). An organization which defines the standards for high-level programming languages, ASCII code, etc.

APL. A simple, compact, interpretive, and easy to learn computer language. Used primarily for applications requiring numerous mathematical operations; particularly well adapted to handling large arrays (matrices). However, it doesn't lend itself to general use and doesn't handle high volumes of data well.

Applications Software. Instructions that tell the computer how to perform a specific function, e.g., inventory control and payroll.

Array. A set of variables which may be arranged within a logical relationship; a table or matrix of data.

ASCII (American Standard Code for Information Interchange). A standard for representing alphanumeric characters in binary (base 2 counting system) patterns. Specific binary patterns represent particular characters and numbers.

Assembly Language. A low-level computer language that uses symbols to represent machine-language instructions.

Auto Indenting. A word-processing function which places every line at a manually preselected tab.

Auto "Normal" Formating. A word-processing system which enters standard text format commands when the system is powered up (turned on).

Back-up. The storage of information on an extra secondary storage medium for protection against physical damage or electrical distortion. Copies of disks, tapes, or paper reports that can be used should an accident or disaster destroy the original data.

Ball. A letter-quality print head that can be changed to achieve different styles of print. Often used with word processing applications.

BASIC (Beginners All-purpose Symbolic Instructional Code). A compact computer language which uses standard English words. A predominantly interpreted language which is dominant in the microcomputer industry.

Baud. A unit of measure for describing the rate at which information passes through a communication line. Baud rate is represented in bits per second. Baud is commonly used to describe the rate at which peripherals such as terminals and printers can send and receive information.

BCD (Binary Code Decimal). A method for representing alphanumerics using bit structures (see ASCII).

Bidirectional. The ability of a word-processing printer to print in both directions: right to left and left to right.

Binary Logic. A method for representing numbers to the base 2. This method of counting uses only symbols 1 and 0. A specified pattern of 1s and 0s can represent numbers that stand for ASCII or BCD codes which, in turn, represent characters.

Bit. The smallest unit of memory in a microcomputer. Physically an on-or-off, yes-or-no state within the computer.

Blocks. In word processing, the ability to identify a section of text for the purpose of deleting, moving, or duplicating it. This function gives the word processor the ability to cut and paste the text. "Blocks" of text can be moved to another location, deleted, or duplicated (transferred).

Boot (Bootstrap). A set of resident instructions usually found in ROM which can be initiated by a manual switch. The instructions tell the computer what to do to start up the hardware.

Branch Instruction. An instruction which causes the processor to jump to another location in the program, that is, to break the normal sequential process of getting the next instruction.

Bubble Memory. A new technology that promises larger memory capacity for less money.

Buffer. A block of memory where the CPU can temporarily put information so that a second piece of equipment that works at a different speed can find the block of memory when it needs the information.

Bug. Slang for a logic error in a program. The reason a program aborts or fails to give the desired results.

Bus. Wires or electrical components that permit electrical signals (information) to travel to different parts of the computer system.

Byte. A unit of measure equal to enough information to describe one letter, number, or character. The technical definition of byte can vary based upon the specific hardware.

Cassette. A tape recorder/player and magnetic tape cartridge used to input information into or record output from the CPU.

CCD (Charge-Coupled Device). A type of memory similar to *Bubble Memory* which may bring the price of large storage down.

Centering. A word-processing function that centers text on a line and is especially useful for positioning titles.

Chaining. A process which allows the user to stack in memory one file on top of another without erasing the previously store file. Chaining allows the user to build a long piece of text from smaller pieces in separate files. Some word processors call this "merging" files.

Chip. An electronic component of a microcomputer.

Clock. A device in the CPU which is used as an internal time reference for coordinating internal opeations.

COBOL (COmmon Business Oriented Language). One of the best known and most widely used business computer languages. Because COBOL is verbose, it's not a popular microcomputer language.

Coding. Writing a program.

COGO (COordinate GeOmetry). Special problem-oriented computer language.

Compile. To translate a high-level programming language into machine code which the computer can understand.

Compiler. A program that translates (compiles) the high-level program into machine code.

Console. An input device resembling a typewriter which is used by the computer operator to communicate instructions to the computer's CPU.

cps (Characters per Second). The numbers of letters, numbers, and symbols a printer produces in one second.

CPU (Central Processing Unit). The "brain" of the microcomputer that performs the arithmetic and logic functions. The CPU controls all computer functions, sends commands to the peripheral devices, and controls access to memory.

CRT (Cathode Ray Tube). A peripheral device resembling a television that displays input and output information.

Cursor. A highlighted mark appearing on the CRT. A bright square or underscore character which indicates where the next entry on the keyboard will be recorded on the CRT.

Cursor Addressing and Sensing. The ability of the computer to locate the position of the cursor and to detect its movement.

Cursor Control. The ability the software gives the user to position the cursor.

Daisy Wheel. The device on many printers that gives the printer the ability to print letter-quality reports and to change print style. A daisy wheel printer is generally durable and more expensive.

Data Base. A large file of organized data which users can draw upon for a common pool of up-to-date information.

Data Base File. The collection of records forming a data base.

DBMS (Data Base Management System). The software system for designing, creating, and subsequently managing a data base, e.g., creating files, editing files, reporting, and sorting files.

Debug. To find and correct a logic error (bug) in a program.

Decibel. A measure of loudness. For printers, 70 db is considered maximum for office use.

Decimal Alignment. The ability of the word processor to line up the decimal points on calculations and figures entered. This is especially useful for applications such as billing and creating monthly reports.

Delete Editing. The ability of a word processor to delete (erase) a specific word or phrase throughout the text with a single command. For example, if the user wants to remove every occurance of the word "Mr.", a single command will accomplish the task throughout the text.

Dictionary. Some word processors use a built-in dictionary of words to check the user's spelling. The misspelled word is highlighted so the user can be alerted and correct the mistake.

Digital. Opposite of analogue; a system or device using discrete signals (usually binary code) to represent numerical data. Almost all computer operations are digital.

Direct Access. The ability of a disk drive to move the read/write head directly to the track on the disk which the computer wishes to access.

Disk Access. The process of retrieving or writing information to the disk by the disk drive. The access time is from 1/10 second to 2 seconds compared to millionths of a second for accessing internal memory.

Disk Drive Unit. A peripheral device that spins a floppy or hard disk and reads information from and writes information to the disk storage media.

Diskette. A flexible disk made of magnetic tape material and used by a disk drive for storing information.

Display. Noun: The picture on the CRT (Cathode Ray Tube—TV type screen). Verb: To transfer information to a peripheral device, e.g., printer or CRT.

Documentation. The manuals describing how to operate equipment and programs. These manuals are essential for training personnel and implementing the computer system.

DOS (Disk Operating System). The set of instructions needed by the computer to operate a disk drive.

Dot Matrix. A printing style which uses small dots to form characters. The results are similar to newspaper print.

Dot Matrix Printer. A printer that uses dot matrix printing style for forming characters.

Dots per Inch (dpi). The density of the dots created by a dot matrix printer. The greater the dpi, the more clear the image.

Double Density. The ability to pack information on a floppy disk at twice the normal capacity.

Dumb Terminal. A terminal that has only basic functions and limited memory.

Dump. The transfer of large amounts of information from main memory to a device like a printer, disk drive, tape, or CRT screen.

Duplex. The ability to transfer information in two directions at one time.

Editing (Error Detection). Protection built in a computer program that tests the data entered by the operator. The computer checks to see if the amounts are reasonable, e.g., MONTH in a numeric date field is less than 13.

Electrostatic Printing. A printing process that forms characters with electrical current on special paper.

Embedded Commands. Formating commands used in word processing which instruct the CRT and printer how to display the text, e.g., centering, tabs, new line, paragraph, line spacing, margins, go to top of next page (top of form), and pause.

Enable. To switch a device on; i.e., setting the processor to accept signals.

Endless Loop. A process which occurs when a branch instruction sends the processor to an earlier statement and causes the routine (portion of the program) to continuously recycle, thus never allowing the program to end.

Enter Key. A key on the keyboard that, when pushed, causes the data previously typed by the user to be transferred through wires to the CPU.

EPROM (Erasable Programmable Read-Only Memory). A PROM which can be erased and reprogrammed with special devices.

Erase. To remove data from memory.

Execute. To run a program.

Executive Program. A program that controls or supervises the execution of other programs or the overall operation of a system.

Exit. To leave one program for another.

Field. The individual factor in a record such as name, address, zip code, or telephone number.

Floppy Disk. A secondary storage medium for information and programs. A thin, mylar, record-shaped disk housed in a protective cardboard jacket. The magnetic surface can store large amounts of information for microcomputer use.

Flow Chart. See *Input/Output Flowchart* and *Logic Flowchart.*

Flush Right. A word-processing command which causes the text to have the right margin justified.

FORTRAN (FORmula TRANslation). A popular language developed for conversion of mathematical formulas into machine code.

Friction Feed. A process of moving paper (scrolling) through a printer while using only the friction between the body and roller. Typewriters are friction feed devices.

Game Paddle. An input peripheral which is popular to computer games. It moves a target (or cursor) on the CRT.

Global Editing. The ability of a word processor to search, find, delete, and replace text.

Go Down. A slang term meaning to stop functioning.

Handshake. Signals or pulses that establish synchronization between an asynchrous I/O unit and the computer.

Handshaking. The signals or pulses that establish synchronization between the disk drive (or other devices) and the computer.

Hard Copy. A slang term for the printed material produced by a computer.

Hard Disk. A metallic, record-shaped disk which is usually hermetically sealed from the environment. The magnetic surface can store large amounts of information for microcomputer use.

Hardware. The equipment or electrical components of a microcomputer.

Headers/Footers. The ability of a word processor to "slug" each page with the title or some identifying message at the top or bottom.

High-Level Language. A computer language which resembles English and needs a compiler or interpreter to translate the program into machine code which the computer can use.

HITS (Hobbyist's Interchange Tape Standard). Data recording standard for cassette tapes.

Hyphenation. To make the word-processing text as attractive as possible, some systems tell the user which words should be hyphenated and allow the user to designate the breaking point. The rules for hyphenation are so complex, it is almost impossible to have a program hyphenate accurately.

IC (Integrated Circuit). A tiny electronic circuit contained in a single silicon chip. A technology that makes microcomputers possible.

ICES (Integrated Civil Engineering System). Special problem-oriented computer language.

Intelligent Terminal. A terminal which has limited memory allowing it to do editing and to store up to eight pages of text.

Initialize. To reset a system to its starting condition; to set various parts of a program so it will behave the same way each time it is repeated. Initializing a disk is accomplished by running a program that prepares the disk for use by the computer. The program also tests for flaws on the disk.

Input. Noun: Information put into the computer. Verb: To put information into the computer.

Input/Output Flowchart. A picture of the action in a program which shows the movement of information to and from the various I/O peripheral devices.

Input Peripheral. Devices such as terminals, consoles, light pens, temperature sensors, disk drives, cassette tape players, and ten-key pads that send signals to the CPU.

Interface. An electrical circuit that connects the computer to a peripheral device, e.g., to a printer.

Interface Controller and Formater. The electronic device that interprets signals from the CPU and which controls the position of the read/write head, formats the data on the disk, and implements handshake routines (programs).

Internal Memory. The electrical circuits within the computer that allow the microcomputer to retain information. The CPU can access internal memory in millionths of a second. The internal memory consists of ROM (*Read-Only Memory*) and RAM (*Random-Access Memory*).

Interpreter. An on-line (immediate) error checking program retained in memory while a program is being written and executed. An interpreter converts high-level language instructions into a code which the machine can understand and execute. Since the interpreter translates the higher-level language, e.g. BASIC, each time the program is run, computer execution of the high-level instructions is relatively slow.

Jargon. Technical computer terms or abbreviations, e.g. DOS, boot, field, file.

Joy Stick. See *Game Paddle.*

K. Abbreviation for kilobyte.

Key. A retrieval code contained in a record, for example surname is a key field in a telephone directory.

Keyboard. A typewriter-type device used to enter information into the computer.

Kilobyte. 1,024 bytes (characters) of information.

Label. Descriptive identifier; group of characters used to describe a file, message, or record.

LCD (Liquid Crystal Display). A technology used for displaying the time on a watch and also used in many computer peripheral devices to display information.

LED (Light Emitting Diode). An electrical component which uses light to provide a digital read-out similar to the time display on a watch (often red).

Light Pen. A photoelectric device which can detect the presence of light at a particular point on a CRT screen. It looks like a pen and has a cable which connects it to a controller. When placed on the screen, the controller detects where the pen is located. Depending on the program, the computer will take appropriate action, for example, the selection of a response or the drawing of a character.

Line Number. Certain programming languages such as FORTRAN and BASIC allow the programmer to assign a line number at the start of each instruction. This number is used by other instructions to identify where execution is to begin next.

Line-Oriented. A line-oriented word processing system allows the cursor to move anywhere on the screen. Also, single lines can be displayed and edited.

Lines per Minute (lpm). The number of lines a printer can print in one minute.

Lisp. A computer language that manipulates non-numerical data efficiently.

Load. To transfer information from peripheral storage into memory or transfer from the memory to secondary storage, e.g. load a program.

Load Module. The output from a compiler. A compiled program in computer executable form.

Log. A written or computer ledger that indicates who uses the computer when, which programs, and how long they execute.

Logic. Systemized interconnection of discrete components in the processor; logic functions include *and, or,* and *not.*

Logic Flowchart. A graphic representation of a system or a program that shows the operations occuring in the central processor.

Logo. A language especially adaptable to learning that follows advanced learning theories.

Loop. A group of instructions in a program that can be executed more than once before the program continues; for example, an incremental counter (keep adding 1 each time this loop is run until the counter reaches 65 and then continue with the program).

Low-Level Language. Machine code and assembly languages which are written in minute detail. They have faster operating speeds but require greater programming skill and patience and are machine-dependent (specific to a particular brand and model of computer).

LSI (Large-Scale Integration). Electrical circuitry with a large number of logic operations per component.

Machine Code. A language that actually addresses the electronic structure of the computer and requires no interpretation. The machine-executable version of a program.

Main Memory. RAM and ROM; the internal memory of a microcomputer which can be accessed very rapidly by the CPU.

Medium. A secondary storage magnetic surface, e.g. tape, floppy disk, and hard disk.

Memory. The circuits or devices that can store informtion for the computer to use.

Menu. A list of choices presented by the software which represents a decision point in the running of the program. The selection of a particular item displayed on the CRT allows the computer to proceed in the desired direction. Menus tend to reduce errors by simplifying operator response.

Menu Driven. A processing style which presents choices to the user before continuing. The user inputs a code to indicate which function is desired.

Merge. The word-processing ability which allows the user to combine two pieces of information from different files. For example, if personalized letters are required in large volume, a mailing list with names and addresses can be combined (merged) with the text of the letter to create personalized letters. Also, some applications require repeated use of specific paragraphs as in legal contracts. These paragraphs can be stored in another file and pulled into the document as needed. Merge implies placing two or more sets of data (records) on one file.

Microcomputer. A small computer.

Microsecond. One millionth of a second (M).

Millisecond. One thousandth of a second.

Mode Control. The number of mode controls determines how efficiently a word processing system operates. Some systems require the user to select *write* (add text), *edit* (change text), or *jump around* (move cursor) before commanding that operation. Other systems allow all of these functions to occur at once without special instructions for mode selection.

MODEM (MOdulator/DEModulator). A device which converts data from the processor to a signal that can be transmitted over communication (telephone) lines. A MODEM also reconverts the data at the receiving end so that the processor can use the information.

MOS (Metal Oxide Semiconductor). Widespread technology used in microcomputers which made LSI possible.

Mother Board. An electronic assembly board on which printed circuits (PC) can be interconnected through a bus.

MPU (MicroProcessor Unit). The electronic circuits in a microcomputer which perform arithmetic and logic functions and control I/O devices. The CPU of a microcomputer.

Nanosecond. One billionth of a second (ns).

Nibble. One half of an 8-bit byte; 4 bits.

Noise. Unwanted electrical signals; interference.

Nonvolatile. The type of memory chip that retains its memory when power is turned off, e.g., ROM and PROM.

Null. Program instruction meaning to do nothing. Null instructions allow time to pass between processing instructions and thus serve to slow down the program execution. Often referred to as CONTINUE or NO-OPERATION Instructions.

Object Code. The output from an interpreter or compiler. The executable version of a program originally written in a high-level language. The code the microprocessor can understand.

Off-Line. Disconnected from the computer or not communicating with the computer; for example a key punch machine is an off-line piece of equipment; if a printer is turned off, it becomes off-line.

On-Line. Connected to and communicating with the computer; for example, a CRT displaying computer output.

Operator Manual. The manual that tells the user how to run the equipment or the operating programs.

Optical Wand. A bar code reader which usually feeds signals into a cassette tape recorder. Used by grocers to read the pricing and inventory information off of packages and containers.

Output. Noun: Information generated by the computer and communicated through wires to an output device. Verb: To send out information from the computer.

Output Peripheral. Devices such as terminals, CRTs, cassette tape recorders, disk drives, printers, control devices (valves, thermostats), and voice generators that receive signals from the CPU.

Overwrite. To store information in a memory location already containing data in such a manner that destroys the original information.

Paddles. See *Game Paddles.*

Page-Oriented. A word-processing system function which allows the cursor to jump to any desired page.

Pagination. The ability of a word processor to automatically number each printed page. Some word processors allow specification of the placement of the number on the page and others put it in a standard location.

Parallel. A wiring connection that allows the transmission of electrically coded information along several pathways at the same time. A standard connection in the microcomputer industry.

Parallel Interface. An electrical pathway which permits the flow of information of all bits in a "word" through the interface at once; a word of 8 bits needs 8 wires in and 8 wires out of the parallel plug or socket; often used with printers; faster than serial interface but cannot travel as far as serial connectors.

Pascal. A modular, high-level language which can be used on many types of microcomputers.

Password. A special word or code that must be keyed into the system before a process will be performed.

Patch. To temporarily modify the software. This is generally accomplished at the machine language level.

PC (Printed Circuit). An electronic circuit constructed on an insulated board. The electronic parts such as transistors and resistors are attached to the board which has metal strips etched (printed) onto it to connect each component. This rigid, wireless construction is compact and easily mass-produced.

PEEK. A BASIC language command which allows the user to read a specified memory address.

Peripheral. An input or output device connected by wires to the CPU to send or receive electrical signals. See *Input Peripheral* and *Output Peripheral*.

Piggyback EPROM. A developmental tool used to design ROM chips.

Pin Feed. A method for scrolling paper through the printer by using pins on a roller. The pins fit into special holes on the right and left margins of the paper and thus prevent slippage of the paper in the printer.

Platen. The plastic, steel, or rubber roller in a friction feed printer similar to a roller in a typewriter.

Plotter. A mechanical device which receives signals from the processor and draws graphs, pictures, etc.

Pointer. A register or accumulator which holds the address of the next memory location to be accessed by the program. Pointers work like a book mark so the computer can "find its place."

POKE. A BASIC languge command which allows the user to write a piece of information into a specified memory address.

Ports. An electrical outlet in the computer; for example, a plug receptor for an I/O device.

Positioner. The arm in the floppy disk drive that moves the read/write head to the proper track on the disk.

Printer. A printing device that makes a hard copy (paper print-out) of the data, programs, or communications from the CPU. Printers are operated by the computer and may have a keyboard.

Printer Formating. This word processing capability allows the user to control the printer for line spacing (single, double, etc.), line width, page length, top and bottom margins, right and left margin justi-fication, proportional spacing, and pausing. Some systems allow the entry of additional text directly from the keyboard after a "pause" command. This permits, for example, the personalization of a letter.

Print Modes. Allows the word processor to command the printer to print continuously to the end of the document, to stop after each page (this allows insertion of stationery), or to stop within the page so text may be added from the keyboard.

Program. Noun: The step-by-step instructions that tell the computer what to do. Verb: To write the instructions for the computer.

Programmer. One who writes instructions (programs) for the computer.

Program Specifications. An outline of what the program is designed to do. Specifications are written before any actual programming steps are written.

PROM (Programmable Read-Only Memory). A type of read-only memory (ROM) which can be programmed by the user.

PROM Burner. A special device used to program a PROM or reprogram an EPROM.

Prompt. Set of instructions that the program displays for the user that tells the user step by step what to do to operate the system. See *Menu Driven.*

Prompted Program. A program which signals the operator what action is required to continue processing.

Protocol. Set of conventions for the exchange of information between I/O devices.

RAM (Random-Access Memory). Chips in the computer that can store and transfer information to and from the CPU. The scratch pad for the CPU where temporary information is stored. RAM is alterable and the information is erased when the computer is turned off.

Read/Write Head. The component of the disk drive that transfers information to and from the hard or floppy disk. Its function is similar to that of a needle on a record player.

Record. A collection of fields forming one unit of data; for example, an employee record.

Record Layout. A diagram of the fields and the space each field will occupy (number of digits), e.g., a field for a telephone number may require 12 digits.

Register. See *Accumulator.*

Removable Cartridge. A type of hard disk that allows the disk to be removed from the disk drive and to be replaced by other disks.

REM Statement. A BASIC language command that allows remarks to be embedded in the program. REM statements are generally used to make notations about what is happening and thus are an aid in debugging or modifying the program. REM is short for *Remarks.*

Replace Editing. The ability of a word processor to edit a specific word or phrase throughout the text with a single command. For example, if the user wants to change the word "paper" to "document" everywhere in the text, a single command will accomplish the task.

Reset. To set the microcomputer to start at the beginning of the program.

Return. See *Enter.*

Reverse Video. The ability of the TV or CRT peripheral to display dark characters on a light background.

ROM (Read-Only Memory). Chips in the computer that are preprogrammed with the basic repetitive instructions to operate the computer. ROM is permanent and not erasable.

Routine. A program within a program. A set of sequential instructions which tells the computer what to do.

RS 232. A wiring connection that allows the transmission of electrically coded information along a single pathway (serial). A standard connection common to the computer industry.

Run. To execute one or more programs.

S 100. 100 pin bus; popular connection; standards for all pin functions are not uniformly defined.

Screen Clear. To erase all data from the CRT.

Screen Formating. This word-processing capability allows the user to visualize the printed format on the screen. Margins can be adjusted to different line widths, page length can be specified, titles are centered, etc.

Screen Load. In word processing, the amount of text the CRT is capable of displaying at one time. Screen load is measured in characters per line and lines per screen. The larger the screen load, the better able the user is to perform format editing.

Scrolling. Page scrolling is the ability to display the text line by line or page by page on the screen. It is particularly useful for proofreading and editing word processing.

Search (Find). The ability of the word processing system to locate every occurance of a word or group of characters in the text. For example, the user might want to *find* "paper" to manually change it to "document" in some instances. The Search and Find commands display each occurance.

Secondary Storage. The information storage devices external to the computer, e.g., floppy disk and cassette tape. Large amounts of information can be retained without consuming the computer's limited memory capacity.

Segregation of Duties. A security precaution that separates the duties of people using a system in such a way that no one person can perform the entire process, such as creating paychecks, or applying cash to accounts receivable.

Serial. A wiring connection that allows the transmission of information along one wire to an output device such as a printer.

Serial Interface. An electrical pathway which permits the flow of information in "single file" through the electrical connections; the binary code travels in sequence or single channel; widely used with printer and terminal connections to the computer; slower than parallel interface and can travel longer distances.

Smart. See *Intelligent Terminal.*

SNOBOL. A computer language that manipulates non-numerical data efficiently.

Software. The instructions that tell the computer what to do and how to do it.

Sort Key. The field used to sort records, for example the surname in a telephone directory.

Source Code. Program written by a programmer usually in a high-level language. The "source" for the object code.

Special Function Keys. Keys on the keyboard which allow the user to utilize more of the computer's capabilities. These keys serve as codes to instruct the computer to do standard functions. For example, *Control R* might cause the cursor to move to the right margin in a word processing system.

Split Screen. The ability to see one part of the text while editing another part on the screen.

Stack. Temporary memory in main memory which automatically keeps track of locations using a stack pointer.

Status. The state of a particular I/O device representing its condition, for example, ready to receive information or ready to send information.

STRESS (STRuctural Engineering Systems Solver). A special problem-oriented computer language.

String. A sequence of records, words, or characters usually in a specific order.

String Variable. A character string treated as a single grouping of characters. For example, a word processing system is able to search for the letters and spaces "RD PRO" which partially form the words "woRD" or "PROcessor" even though the characters are not distinct English words.

Subroutine. A small portion of a program which performs a specific operation.

Swapping. A process for reading in only a portion of a program from secondary storage and putting it back on the disk when the next segment is required to continue. This process saves space in RAM. See *Virtual Memory.*

Syntax. The rules which describe how programming language statements must be constructed, i.e., the grammer of the computer language.

Systems Manual. The manual that describes how an entire system works. The overview or umbrella for the other manuals.

Systems Software. The computer executable instructions that tell the computer how to communicate, how to relate to the peripherals (printer, terminal, etc.), and how to operate internally.

Tape. Magnetic recording tape which the computer can write information to and read from.

Terminal. The combination of keyboard and CRT or television monitor.

Thermal Printing. A printing process that uses heat to activate heat-sensitive paper thus creating a character.

Thimble Printing. See *Ball* and *Daisy Wheel.*

Throughput Rate. The operating speed with which a computer processes data and produces a result.

Time Sharing. Simultaneous use of the computer by two or more users. The processor handles the demands sequentially at a speed that is so fast that it appears to be simultaneous.

Track. Defined area on a disk where information is stored. Tracks are arranged in concentric circles on the disk.

Tractor Feed. A method similar to pin feed which moves paper through a printer. The tractor is adjustable to different paper widths and often removable.

Trap. A method for finding program errors.

True Descenders. A printing style where the tails of letters such as *y, j, g,* etc. descend below the word.

Unconditional Branch. A jump in the program instructions which is always taken.

User. A person who uses computer-generated information or reports.

User Manual. The manual that tells what information must be entered, how output reports are formated, and what functions a particular program will perform.

Verification. A method for checking input data to make sure it is entered correctly. For example, a check to see if the data is entered as alpha or numeric characters. See *Editing.*

Vertical Centering. A word-processing ability which locates the text on the page evenly from top to bottom.

Virtual Memory. An operating system technique which automatically transfers program sections or data between the disk and main memory; a method for increasing effective memory capacity of the computer. See *Swapping.*

VLSI. Very Large Scale Integration.

Wrap Around. A word-processing ability which allows the user to type continuously without striking the *return* key at the end of each line. The word processor automatically formats the text margins at the time it is displayed on the screen or on the printer.

INDEX

A

Abort, 169
Access, 68, 70, 74, 75, 76, 77, 80, 116
Access time, 70, 80
Accumulator, 100
Address, 100
Alphanumeric, 150
ALU (see also CPU), 101
American National Standards Institute (ANSI), 101, 133, 186, 189
American Standard Code for Information Interchange (ASCII), 193
Analogue, 101
ANSI, 101
APL, 156, 158, 159
Applications, 12–61, 113, 114, 116, 154, 158
  amortization, 46
  androids, 40

Applications (*cont.*)
  animation, 28, 41
  architecture, 36–37
  astronomy, 17
  banking, 19
  biofeedback. 17
  biorhythm, 17
  business, 35–47
  Computer-Aided Adult Learning (CAAL), 31
  Computer Assisted Instruction (CAI), 30
  Computer Augmented Learning (CAL), 30
  Computer Managed Instruction (CMI), 30
  control, 15, 43, 44
  construction, 44
  diet, 37
  disabled, 15
  drill and practice
    (see also Education applications), 22, 27, 30

Applications (*cont.*)
  education (see also Education applications), 25–33
  energy, 18, 40, 44
  engineering, 42, 43
  financial records, 46
  forecasting, 39
  games, 16, 19–20, 41, 129–34
  genealogy, 22
  graphics, 28, 30, 40–41, 132, 138, 141
    slides, 30
  information retrieval, 45
  insurance, 20
  investments, 18, 19, 39, 44, 46
  inventory, 20, 46, 47
  home, 11–23
  lasers, 44
  library, 16, 19
  literacy (see also Education), 22, 27, 30
  mail, 16, 20, 42, 45
  membership list, 14
  models (see also Forecasting, Simulation), 28, 142
  music, 17, 43
  newsletter, 13
  personnel, 37–38
  photography, 42
  production, 47
  reservations, 39
  robots, 40, 155
  safety, 43
  security, 15, 161–66
  simulation, 28, 29, 42, 43
  skills inventory, 20
  slides, 40–41
  software, 56, 111, 112, 116, 147, 150, 179, 189
  taxes, 21, 45
  telecommunications, 12, 16, 18, 39, 40
  training (see also Education Applications), 25–33, 29
  typesetting, 44
  user group (club), 23, 133
  voice synthesis, 15
  weather, 42
  writing, 21
  word processing (see also Word processing), 13, 21
Arithmetic Logic Unit (ALU), 101
Array, 158, 169
ASCII, 193
Assembler, 155, 157, 158
Assembly language, 155
Auto indenting (see Word processing)
Auto "normal" formatting (see Word processing)

Auxiliary memory (see Secondary storage)

B

Back-up (see also Security), 75, 77, 78, 80, 163, 164, 166, 186
Ball (see also Printer), 85
BASIC, 147, 148, 155, 156, 157
  interpreter, 148, 155, 156, 157, 158, 159
  PEEK, 169
  POKE, 169
Baud (see also Communications), 94, 96, 101
Baud rate (see Baud)
BCD (Binary Code Decimal), 101
Beginners All-purpose Symbolic Instructional Code (see BASIC)
Bidirectional (see also Printer), 88, 89
Binary (see Binary logic), 101
Binary Code Decimal (BCD), 101
Binary logic, 101
Bit, 67, 74, 75, 80, 96
Blocks (see Word processing)
Boot, 68, 70, 142, 169
Bootstrap (see Boot)
Boostrap program (see Boot)
Branch instruction (see also Program), 169
Bubble memory, 69, 70
Buffer, 69, 70, 101
Bug (see also Debug), 127, 128
Bus, 101
Business Applications (see also Applications), 35–48
Byte, 66, 70, 77, 80, 96

C

Calculator, 4
Cassette player/recorder, 6, 75, 80, 186, 189
Cassette tape, 6, 74, 80, 90, 111, 116, 132–34, 163, 186, 187
Cathode Ray Tube (see CRT)
CCD, 69, 70
Centering (see Word processing) Central file, 50
Central Processing Unit (see CPU)
Charge-coupled device (CCD), 69, 70
Chaining (see Word processing)
Characters per line (see also Printer), 93
Characters per second (see also cps), 88, 89
Chip, 67, 70, 94, 96
  EPROM, 69, 71
  memory, *Figure 1–1*, 5, 7, 71, 81
  PROM, 68, 71
  RAM (see also Internal memory), *Figure 1–1*, 5, 8, 117
  ROM, 8, 117, 181

Clock, 5, 6
COBOL (COmmon Business Oriented Language), 147, 148, 150, 156, 157, 158, 159
Code (see also Coding, Program), 148, 150, 170
Coding (see also Code, Program), 150
COGO (COordinate GeOmetry), 158, 159
Common Business Oriented Language (see COBOL)
Communications, 94, 96, 101
  baud, 94, 96, 101
  MODEM, 102
Compile, 148, 150
Compiler, 155, 156, 157, 158, 159
  object code, 155, 158, 159, 169
  source code, 170
Console (see Terminal)
CP/M (see Disk operating system)
cps, 88, 89
CPU, 5, 6, 7, 68, 70, 80, 111, 116, 189
  accumulator, 100
  ALU, 101
  clock, 5, 6
  logic, 102
CRT (see also Screen), 6, 7, 55, 56, 57, 82, 83, 92, 93, 96, 102, 132, 186, 189
  display, 102, 133
  reverse video, 94, 96
Cursor, 57, 94, 96, 140, 142
Cursor addressing and sensing, 94
Cursor control, 57

D

Daisy wheel (see also Printer), 85, 89
Data base, 49–52, 127, 128, 155, 179, 181
Data base file, 52
Data Base Management System (DBMS), 49–52
Debug (see also Bug), 127, 128, 148, 150, 151, 158, 159, 179, 181
Decibel (see also Printer), 88, 89
Decimal alignment (see Word processing)
Delete editing (see Word processing)
Dictionary (see Word processing)
Digital, 101
Direct access (see also Disk drive unit), 80
Disk access (see also Disk drive unit), 116
Disk drive unit, 7, 71, 72, 76, 80, 185, 189
  controller, 77
  disk access, 116
  direct access, 80
  Disk Operating System (DOS), 80, 112, 149, Figure 7–1

positioner, 71, 77, 81
  read/write head, 72, 76, 77, 111
Diskette, Figure 8–1, 5–9, 71–72, 74, 78, 80, 111, 116, 132, 133, 156, 163, 186, 187
  floppy disk, 5–9, Figure 8–1, 71, 74, 80, 116, 189
  double density, 77, 80
  track, 72, 81
Disk operating system (DOS) (see also Disk drive unit), 80, 112, 149, Figure 7–1
Display (see also CRT and Screen), 102, 133
Documentation, 119–28, 148, 150, 188–89
  evaluation of, 119–28
  manuals, 114, 121
  operating manual, 148, 158, 187
  systems, 128, 187, 190
  redundancy, 128
  routing, 127
  users, 6, 8, 121, 128, 133, 141, 187, 190
DOS (see also Disk drive unit), 80, 112, 149, Figure 7–1
Dot matrix (see also Printer), 85, 89, 187, 189, Figure 9–1
Dots per inch (dpi), 89
Double density (see also Diskette), 77, 80
Dumb terminal (see also Terminal), 92, 94, 96
Duplex, 102

E

Editing (see also Verification), 114, 116, 149, 150, 170
Educational software, 135–43
Education applications, 25–33
  art, 32
  attendance records, 32
  automechanics, 32
  chemistry, 31
  drafting, 32
  drill and practice, 33
  eye-hand coordination, 32
  feedback (see also Feedback), 33
  geography, 31
  illustration, 32
  interior decorating, 32
  library, 32
  literacy, 33
  mechanical models, 31
  music, 32
  newspaper, 31
  poetry, 31
  scheduling classes, 32
  software, 135–43
  student records, 32

Education applications (*cont.*)
  three R's, 32
  typing, 31
  weather, 31
  writing, 31
  word processing, 31
Electrostatic printing (see also Printer), 85, 89
Embedded commands (see Word processing)
Enable, 102
Endless loop, 169
Enter (key), 7, 8, 139
EPROM, 69, 71
Erase, 5, 7
Error code, 123
Error detection (see also Editing), 114, 116, 149, 150, 170
Error statement, 148
Execute, 120, 128
Executive program, 169
Exit, 170
External storage (see Secondary storage)

F

Feedback, 33
  active, 137
  interactive, 137
  negative, 138
  passive, 137
Field (see File)
File (see also Data base management)
  field, *Figure 5–1*, 51, 52, 114, 147, *Figure 16–1*, 150, 151, 181
  sort, 170
  record, *Figure 5–1*, 51, 52, 147, 150–52, 181
    label, 169
    layout, *Figure 16–1*
Firmware (see also ROM and EPROM), 9, 111
Floppy disk (see Diskette)
Flow chart, 147, 179, 181
  input/output, 147, 148, *Figure 16–2*
  logic, *Figure 20–1*, 102
  symbols, *Figure 20–2*
Flush right (see Word processing)
FORTRAN (FORmula TRANslation), 147, 158
Friction feed (see also Printer), 87, 89

G

Game paddle, 102, 140, 143
Games, 16, 19–20, 41, 129–34
Global editing (see Word processing)

Go down, 78, 80, 166
Graphics (see also Applications), 28, 30, 40–41, 138, 141

H

Handshake (see also Interface), 71, 102
Hard copy, 89, 111, 187
Hard disk, 7, 64, 72, 74, 75, 77, 78, 80, 81, 111, 116
  removable cartridge, 72, 78, 81
Hardware (see also CRT, Cassette recorder/player, Disk drive unit, Terminal, MODEM, Keyboard, Diskette, Hard disk), 69, 99–105, 110, 111, 120, 121, 156, 186, 181, 189
Header/Footer (see Word processor)
HELP, 135
High-level language, 155, 156, 157, 158, 159
HITS (Hobbiest's Interchange Tape Standard), 102

I

IC (see Integrated circuit), 102
ICES, 159
Information retrieval (see also Data base management), 45
Initialize, 143, 148, 169
Input, *Figure 1–1*, 7
Input/output flow chart (see also Flow chart), 147, 148, *Figure 16–2*
Input peripheral (see also Peripheral), *Figure 1–1*, 7, 68, 70, 71, 81, 147, 151
Instruction (see also Program), 111
Integrated Circuit (IC), 102
Intelligence, 96
Intelligent terminal (see also Terminal), 40, 94, 96
Interface (see also Handshake), 84, 88, 89, 90, 104, 187, 189
  controller formater, 71, 81
  parallel, 88, 89, 102
  RS 232, 90, 104
  S-100, 104
Internal memory, *Figure 1–1. Figure 7–1*, 5, 7, 52, 71, 74, 81, 111, 112, 113, 116, 156, 159, 185
  main memory, 70, 71, 81
  RAM—Random Access Memory (see also Internal memory), *Figure 1–1*, 5, 8, 117
  ROM (Read-Only Memory), 8, 117, 181
Interpreter, 148, 155, 156, 157, 158, 159
  BASIC, 147, 148, 155, 156, 157
Inventory, 20, 46, 47

J

Jargon, 121, 122, 128
Joystick (see Game paddle), 102, 140, 143

K

K (see Kilobyte)
Key, 169
  enter (key), 7, 8, 139
  return, 7, 8, 139
  ten-key pad, 95
  touch, 95, 97
  sort, 170
  special function, 94, 96
Keyboard (see also Terminal), 6, 27, 56, 58,
    92, 95, 96, 141, 186, 187, 189
Kilobyte (K), 66, 71, 81, 112, 113, 116

L

Label (see also File), 169
Language, 66, 113, 150, 153–60, *Figure 7–1*
  APL, 156, 158, 159
  assembly, 155
  BASIC, 147, 148, 155, 156, 157
  binary code, 101
  code, 148, 150, 170
  COBOL, 147, 148, 150, 156, 157, 158, 159
  COGO, 158, 159
  high-level, 155, 156, 157, 158, 159
  ICES, 159
  Lisp, 158–59
  LOGO, 157–59
  low-level, 155, 158
  machine, 155, 158, 159
  Pascal, 156–159
  SNOBOL, 158, 160
  STRESS, 158, 160
LCD (Liquid Crystal Display), 102, 133
LED (Light Emitting Diode), 102
Light pen, 102, 140, 143
Line number (see also Program), 169
Lines per minute (see also Printer), 88, 89
Line-oriented (see Word processor)
Lisp, 158–59
Load, 7, 48, 71, 75, 81, 111, 116, 186, 190
Load module, 156
Log (see also Security), 165, 166
Logic, 102, *Figure 20-1*
Logic error (see Bug, Debug), 127, 155
Logic flowchart (see also Flowchart), *Figure
    20-1*, 151
LOGO, 157–59
Loop, 169

Low-level language, 155, 158
LSI (Large Scale Integration), 102

M

Machine code (see also Object code), 155,
    158, 159, 169
Machine language (see Machine code, Object
    code), 155, 158, 159, 169
Main memory (see also Internal memory),
    70, 71, 81
Mainframe computer, 29, 37, 40
Maintenance, program, 150
Manuals (see Documentation)
Matrix (see also Array), 158, 159
Medium (storage), 71, 75, 81
Memory
  auxiliary (see Secondary storage)
  bubble, 69, 70
  buffer, 69, 70, 101
  erase, 5, 7
  internal (see Internal memory)
  main (see Internal memory)
  nonvolatile, 69, 71
  secondary storage (see Secondary storage)
  volatile (see also Nonvolatile), 69, 71
Menu, 116, 139, 140, 143
Menu driven, 116, 139, 140, 141, 143, 150,
    187
Merge (see Word processor)
Microsecond, 102
Microcomputer, *Figure 1–1*, 3–8
Millisecond, 102
Mode control (see Word processor)
Monitor (see also CRT), 66, 92, 96, 112, 165,
    186, 187
MODEM (MOdulator/DEModulator) (see
    also Communications), 102
MOS, 102
Mother board, 102
MPU (see also CPU), 102

N

Nanosecond, 102
Needs analysis, 28, 173–81
Nibble, 102
Noise, 102
Nonvolatile, 69, 71
Null, 169

O

Object code (see also Compiler), 155, 158,
    159, 169

Off-line (see also Peripheral), 102
On-line (see also Peripheral), 102
Operating system, disk (DOS), *Figure 7–1*, 80, 112, 149
Operator manual (see Users Documentation)
Optical wand, 102
Output, *Figure 1–1*, 7, 190
Output peripheral (see Peripheral)
Overwrite, 102

P

Paddles (see also Game paddles), 102, 140, 143
Page oriented (see Word processor)
Pagination (see Word processor)
Paper feed (see also Printer), 84, 87
Parallel interface (see also Interface), 88, 89, 102
Pascal, 156–159
Password (see also Security), 164, 165, 166
Patch, 169
PC (Printed Circuit), 102
PEEK, 169
Peripheral, *Figure 1-1*, 7, 68–70, 71, 81, 147, 151
   input (see also Cassette player/recorder, Disk drive unit, Game paddle, Keyboard, Hard disk, Light pen, and Optical wand), *Figure 1–1*, 6, 7, 84, 185, 189
   input/output (see also Cassette player/recorder, Disk drive unit, and Hard disk), *Figure 1–1*, 185
   off-line, 102
   on-line, 102
   output (see also CRT, Cassette player/recorder, Disk drive unit, Hard disk, Plotter, and Printer), *Figure 1–1*, 6
Piggyback EPROM (see also EPROM), 69, 71
Pin feed (see also Printer), 85, 87, 89
Platen (see also Printer), 87, 89
Plotter, 102
Pointer (see also Stack), 102
POKE, 169
Portability (see also Pascal), 157
Ports, 102
Positioner (see also Disk drive unit), 71, 77, 81
Power up, 69
Printer, 6, 7, 56, 69, 83–88, 187, 190
   ball, 85
   bidirectional, 88, 89
   characters per line, 93
   characters per second, 88, 89
   daisy wheel, 85, 89
   decibel, 88, 89
   dot matrix, 85, 89, 187, 189, *Figure 9–1*
   dots per inch (dpi), 89
   electrostatic, 85, 89
   friction feed, 87, 89
   lower-case, 55, 56
   head, print, 89
   hard copy, 89, 111, 187
   impact, 85
   letter-quality, 55, 85, 187, *Figure 9–2*
   lines per minute, 88, 89
   paper feed (see also Friction, Pin, and Tractor), 84, 87
   pin feed, 85, 87, 89
   platen, 87, 89
   terminal, 185
   thermal, 85, 89, 90
   true descenders, 85, 90, 94, 97, *Figure 9–2*
   tractor feed, 85, 87, 90
   upper-case, 56, 85, 95
Program, 36, 48, 75, 111, 113, 116, 128, 133, 141, 143, 145–51, 165, 166, 187
   branching instruction, 169
   boot, 68, 70, 142, 169
   bootstrap (see Boot)
   bug (see also Debug), 127, 128
   canned, 113
   coded, 148
   debug, 127, 128, 148, 150, 151, 158, 159, 179, 181
   documentation (see also Documentation), 119–28, 148, 150, 188–89
   editing (error detection), 114, 116, 149, 150, 170
   endless loop, 169
   execute, 120, 128
   executive, 169
   exit, 170
   games, 133
   high-level language, 157
   line numbers, 169
   logic error (see Bug, Debug), 127, 155
   loop, 169
   low-level language, 155, 158
   manuals (see Documentation)
   maintenance, 150
   menu driven, 116, 139, 140, 141, 150, 153, 187
   prompted (see also Menu driven), 116, 163, 187
   routine, 111, 117, 128
   subroutine, 149, 150, 151
   specifications, 146, 148, 151
   unconditional branch, 170
Programmer, 7, 47, 179

Programming, 145–51, 179, 185
  embedded commands (see Word process-
    ing), 59
  language (see Language)
  syntax, 155, 160, 170
PROM, 68, 71
PROM burner, 68, 69, 72
Prompt, 116, 134, 140, 142, 163, 166, 187
Prompted program (see also Menu driven),
    116, 163, 187, 188
Protocol (see also Handshaking), 104

R

RAM (see also Internal memory), *Figure 1–1*,
    5, 8, 117
Read/write head (see also Disk drive unit), 72,
    76, 77, 111
Record (see also File), *Figure 5–1*, 51, 52, 147,
    150–52, 181
Record layout (see also File), *Figure 16–1*
Register (see Accumulator)
Removable cartridge, 72, 78, 81
REM statement, 148, 150
Replace editing (see Word processor)
Reset (see also Boot, Initialize), 141, 142, 169
Return (see Enter key)
Reverse video (see also CRT and Screen), 94,
    96
ROM (see also Internal memory), 8, 117, 181
Routine (see also Program), 111, 117, 128
RS 232 (see also Interface), 90, 104
Run, 169

S

S-100 (see also Interface), 104
Screen (see also CRT), *Figure 7–1*, 56, 96
  clear, 170
  formating, 58
  split, 57
Scrolling, 57
Secondary storage, 70–81, 111, 117, 186, 187
  auxiliary memory, 6
  cassette tape (see Cassette tape)
  disk drive (see Disk drive unit)
  Diskette (see Diskette)
  hard copy, 89, 111, 187
  hard disk (see Hard disk)
  tape (see Cassette tape)
  virtual memory, 170
Security, 161–166
  back-up, 75, 77, 78, 80, 163, 164, 166, 186
  log, 165, 166
  password, 164, 165, 166

Security (*cont.*)
  segregation of duties, 164, 166
Serial interface (see Interface)
SNOBOL, 158, 160
Software, 4, 8, 36, 69, 109–17, 120, 132–34,
    136, 137, 141, 142, 156, 167–70, 174,
    179, 181, 185, 190
  applications (see Applications software)
  DOS, *Figure 7–1*, 80, 112, 149
  educational (see Educational software)
  games (see also Games), 131
  operating system, *Figure 7–1*, 80, 112, 149
  systems, 128, 187, 190
Sort key, 170
Source code (see also High-level language),
    170
Stack (see also Pointer), 102
STRESS, 158, 160
String, 170
String variable, 170
Subroutine (see also Routine), 149, 150, 151
Swapping (see also Virtual memory), 170
Symbols, Flowchart, *Figure 20–2*
Syntax, 155, 160, 170
Synchronize, 76
System, operating (see DOS), *Figure 7–1*, 80,
    112, 149
Systems documentation (see also Documen-
    tation), 128, 187, 190
Systems manual (see also Documentation),
    128, 187, 190
Systems software (see also Software), 134,
    147, 150, 189, 190

T

Tape (see Cassette tape)
Telecommunications, 12, 16, 18, 39, 40
Terminal, 6–8, 78, 91–97, 187, 190
  controls, 94
  CRT, 6, 7, 55, 56, 57, 82, 83, 92, 93, 96,
    132, 186, 189
  delete key, 96, 141
  dumb (low end), 92, 94, 96
  intelligent (smart), 40, 94, 96
  keyboard (see Keyboard)
  screen (see also Screen), *Figure 7–1*, 56, 96
Thermal printing (see also Printer), 85, 89, 90
Thimble (see also Printer), 90
Throughput rate, 208
Time share, 208
Track (see also Diskette), 72, 81
Tractor feed (see also Printer), 85, 87, 90
Trap, 170
True descenders, 85, 90, 94, 97, *Figure 9–2*

BELMONT COLLEGE LIBRARY

U

Unconditional branch (see also Program), 170
User, 6, 8, 121, 128, 133, 141, 187, 190
Users documentation (see also Documentation), 128, 141, 187, 190
Users manual (see Users documentation)

V

Variable, string, 170
Verification (see also Editing, Error code), 114, 116, 149, 150, 170
Vertical centering (see Word processor)
Virtual memory (see also Secondary storage), 170
VLSI (Very Large Scale Integration), 102
Volatile (see also Nonvolatile), 69, 71

W

Word processing, 53–61, 155, 163, 187
  auto indenting, 58
  auto "normal" formating, 58
  blocks, 59
  boldface printing, 60
  centering, 58
  chaining, 58
  codes, 59
  decimal alignment, 60
  dedicated, 54, 56
  delete (erase), 58
  delete editing, 58, 59
  dictionary, 59

Word Processing (cont.)
  embedded commands, 59
  file (security), 61
  find command, 58
  flush right, 58
  footer, 60
  global editing, 59
  glossary, 59
  header, 60
  hyphenation, 60
  invisible lines, 60
  jump around, 57
  line oriented, 57
  local editing, 58
  mathematical calculations, 60
  menu, 59
  merging (see also Chaining), 59
  mode control, 57
  page-oriented, 57
  pagination, 60
  paragraph indenting, 58
  printer formatting, 58
  print mode, 60
  replace editing, 58
  search (find), 58
  screen load, 57
  strikeover, 58
  subscript, 60
  superscript, 60
  tab, 58
  underlining, 60
  vertical centering, 58
  wrap around, 57
  write, 57
Wrap around (see Word processing)